Study Guide
Gaetan T. Giannini, MBA
Cedar Crest College. Pennsylvania

Business in Action
with Real-Time Updates
Fourth Edition

Courtland L. Bovée
John V. Thill

PEARSON
Prentice
Hall

Upper Saddle River, New Jersey 07458

VP/Publisher: Natalie E. Anderson
AVP/Executive Editor: Jodi McPherson
Editorial Project Manager: Claudia Fernandes
Production Project Manager: Lynne Breitfeller
Operations Specialist: Natacha St. Hill Moore

Pearson Prentice Hall™ **is a trademark of Pearson Education, Inc.**

10   9   8   7   6   5   4   3   2   1

ISBN-13: 978-0-13-600410-3
ISBN-10:   0-13-600410-5

Table of Contents

PREFACE

An introductory course in business can teach you quite a bit about how people in business think, speak, act, react, and make decisions. The textbook, the teacher, and the interaction of students eager to learn all contribute to the educational process. This Study Guide is part of that process. If utilized effectively, this Study Guide will aid you in learning the material in *Business in Action with Real-Time Updates*, 4th Edition, by Courtland L. Bovée and John V. Thill.

This Study Guide is designed and written to reinforce your learning from the textbook, class lectures, and class discussions. The objectives of this Study Guide are

1. To provide you with the materials that will be useful in learning the business vocabulary and business concepts presented in your text.

2. To provide you with an opportunity to test your understanding of what you have read, studied, and learned.

3. To help you prepare for quizzes and examinations by testing yourself with sample exam-type questions.

4. To encourage you to apply your understanding of the business concepts presented in the text to interesting, real-world business problems and opportunities.

These goals are achieved through a variety of exercises and problems. Each chapter begins with specific Learning Objectives and then presents objective questions in the form of True-False questions, Multiple Choice questions, and Match the Terms and Concepts with Their Definitions. Subjective questions such as Critical Thinking questions and Exploring the Internet will also be asked. All these activities combine to test your understanding and recall of chapter content. The following is an effective study program for making best use of these aids:

1. Read the statement of objectives at the beginning of each chapter in the Study Guide.
2. Begin answering the True-False, Multiple Choice, and Matching Key Terms portions of the Study Guide. If you have any trouble with any of these sections, keep referring to the textbook until you feel comfortable. Remember that each chapter contains an Answers section after the questions and exercises that you can use to check your answers as you go. Immediate feedback is essential for success in the learning process.
3. Complete all other sections of the chapter. Make certain you feel confident in your knowledge of the material before going on to the next chapter.

Don't let anything in this course overwhelm or discourage you. If you tackle the textbook, the Study Guide, and the course chunks at a time and follow the suggested program above, you will gain the practice and resulting skills necessary to become an effective business student.

The Organization of this Study Guide

Each chapter in this Study Guide is arranged in the following order:

LEARNING OBJECTIVES
You should be able to accomplish these learning objectives after studying the chapter and working through the Study Guide.

TRUE-FALSE
These true-false questions will be very similar to the types of true-false questions found on your exams (if your professor gives these types of questions—ask whether that is the case). Even if your professor does not ask these types of questions on the exams, you are still strongly encouraged to work through this section. To increase your learning, you are asked to correct any false statements by making them true statements. The answers for this section, as well as all others, are provided at the end of the chapter.

MULTIPLE CHOICE
These multiple choice questions will be very similar to those you find on your exams—especially considering that many professors give multiple choice type exams. Choose the best answer from the options provided. You are strongly encouraged to correct the incorrect responses to make them correct. By doing so, you will come to recognize the subtle differences between potential answers. This is a skill required to be successful in performing well on multiple choice type exams.

MATCH THE TERMS AND CONCEPTS WITH THEIR DEFINITIONS
This section is important because many test questions will ask you to define a term or a concept. Moreover, learning the language of business is half the task to understanding business.

LEARNING OBJECTIVES—SHORT ANSWER OR ESSAY QUESTIONS
Many of you will have professors that will give you short answer and/or essay type questions. If so, then this section will be particularly useful to you. Even if you do not expect these types of questions on exams, you are still strongly encouraged to work through this section. It will help you accomplish the learning objectives of this chapter.

CRITICAL THINKING QUESTIONS
These questions are designed to elicit a higher level of thinking by requiring you to pull together various concepts introduced in the chapter.

EXPLORING THE INTERNET

This section is provided in some of the chapters and consists of one question that instructs you to go to the Internet and find out more information about a topic. This activity will allow you to discover current information and will give you ideas of great resources for your future. As with the other activities, an answer is provided at the end of the chapter.

ANSWERS

The final section of each chapter provides the answers to all of the exercises.

Good luck!

I would like to thank Rebecca Getz of Cedar Crest College for her assistance in compiling this Study Guide.

Gaetan T. Giannini, MBA

Chapter 1
The Fundamentals of Business and Economics

Think of this Study Guide as your tutor. It is designed to give you more practice and familiarity with terminology and concepts discussed in the textbook. Be sure to read and study each chapter carefully before attempting these exercises. (Answers are found at the end of each chapter.)

Learning Objectives
After reading this chapter, you should be able to:

1. Define what a business is and identify four vital social and economic contributions that businesses make.
2. Differentiate between goods-producing and service businesses, and list five factors contributing to the increase in the number of service businesses.
3. Differentiate between a free-market system and a planned system.
4. Explain how supply and demand interact to affect price.
5. Discuss the four major economic roles of the U.S. government.
6. Explain how a free-market system monitors its economic performance.
7. Identify five challenges you will face as a business professional in the coming years.

True-False
Indicate whether the statement is generally true or false by placing a "T" or an "F" in the space provided. If it is a false statement, correct it so that it becomes a true statement.

_____ 1. A business is any profit-seeking organization that provides goods and services designed to satisfy customers' needs.

_____ 2. Nonprofit organizations are regular companies that attempt to make a profit but fail to do so.

_____ 3. Technologies often included under the Web 2.0 umbrella include blogging, podcasting, wikis, newsfeeds, tagging, and virtual worlds.

_____ 4. Because they require large amounts of money, equipment, land, and other resources to get started and to operate, goods-producing businesses are often labor-intensive businesses.

_____ 5. Rather than creating tangible goods, service businesses perform activities for customers.

_____ 6. Over the past few decades, the U.S. economy has undergone a profound transformation from being dominated by manufacturing to being dominated by services.

_____ 7. Capitalism and private enterprise are the terms most often used to describe a planned system.

_____ 8. At the equilibrium price point, customers are willing to buy as many products as companies are willing to sell.

_____ 9. In an oligopoly there is only one supplier of a product in a given market, and that supplier thus is able to determine the price.

_____ 10. Antitrust laws limit what businesses can and cannot do to ensure that all competitors have an equal chance of producing a product, reaching the market, and making a profit.

_____ 11. Economic contraction occurs when spending declines, businesses cut back on production, employees are laid off, and the economy as a whole slows down.

_____ 12. The discount rate is the interest rate the Federal Reserve charges commercial banks to borrow money.

_____ 13. Statistics that signal a swing in the economy after the movement has begun are called leading indicators.

_____ 14. When the inflation rate begins to decline, economists use the term *disinflation*.

Multiple Choice
Circle the best answer for each of the following questions.

1. Which of the following is an acceptable use of the term *business*?
   a. As a label for the overall field of business concepts, as in "I plan to major in business"
   b. As a collective label for the activities of many companies, as in "This legislation is viewed as harmful to American business"
   c. As a synonym for company, as in "Apple is a successful business"
   d. All of the above

2. Which of the following is not a way that business contributes to society?
   a. Providing necessities such as housing, clothing, food, transportation, communication, health care, and much more
   b. Lobbying Congress to ensure that its needs are being met
   c. Pay taxes that fund government services that benefit society, such as transportation infrastructure, education, and scientific research
   d. Reinvesting its profits in the economy, thereby creating a higher standard of living and quality of life for society as a whole

3. For a capital-intensive business, which of the following factors can be considered a barrier to entry?
   a. Strict licensing procedures
   b. Unlimited labor supply
   c. Limited supply of raw materials
   d. Both a and c

4. Which of the following is not a reason for the growth of the service business sector?
   a. Colleges are offering more service-oriented degrees
   b. Many consumers have more disposable income
   c. Services are needed to support complex goods and new technology
   d. Companies are increasingly seeking professional advice

5. Which of the following is not one of the five factors of production?
   a. Natural resources
   b. Entrepreneurship
   c. Economics
   d. Knowledge

6. Which of the following is not a type of planned economic system?
   a. Communism
   b. Capitalism
   c. Socialism
   d. Both b and c

7. Of the following, which factor would not contribute to increasing the demand for a product?
   a. Increasing customer income
   b. The introduction of a substitute product
   c. Improved customer preferences toward the product
   d. An increase in product-marketing expenditures

8. Supply of a product is affected by all of the following except:
   a. An increase in product-marketing expenditures
   b. Cost of inputs (wages, raw material, etc.)
   c. Number of competitors
   d. Advancements in technology

9. When markets become filled with competitors and products start to look alike, companies use which of the following to gain a competitive advantage?
    a. Price and speed
    b. Quality and service
    c. Innovation and convenience
    d. All of the above

10. Antitrust laws are not designed to ensure that companies have an equal chance of:
    a. Producing a product
    b. Reaching the market
    c. Raising capital
    d. Making a profit

11. The following are examples of a business's stakeholders:
    a. Employees and supervisors
    b. Competitors and their suppliers
    c. Both a and d
    d. Customers, suppliers, and society at large

12. A recession is:
    a. Two consecutive quarters of decline in the gross domestic product
    b. A period of growth in gross national product
    c. A term referring to economic expansion
    d. A measure of a country's economic output

13. Of the following, which is not a type of price index?
    a. API
    b. CPI
    c. PPI
    d. None of the above

14. As world markets continue to globalize, managers and entrepreneurs will have to:
    a. Produce quality goods and services that satisfy customers' changing needs.
    b. Think globally and embrace a culturally diverse workforce.
    c. Neither a or b
    d. Both a and b

Match the Terms and Concepts with Their Definitions

A. barrier to entry
B. business
C. business cycles
D. capital
E. capital-intensive businesses
F. capitalism
G. communism

H. competition
I. competitive advantage
J. consumer price index (CPI)
K. deflation
L. demand
M. demand curve
N. economic indicators

O.	economic system	FF.	monopolistic competition
P.	economics	GG.	monopoly
Q.	entrepreneurship	HH.	natural resources
R.	equilibrium price	II.	nonprofit organizations
S.	fiscal policy	JJ.	oligopoly
T.	free-market system	KK.	planned system
U.	globalization	LL.	privatization
V.	goods-producing businesses	MM.	producer price index (PPI)
W.	gross domestic product (GDP)	NN.	profit
X.	gross national product (GNP)	OO.	pure competition
Y.	human resources	PP.	recession
Z.	inflation	QQ.	recovery
AA.	knowledge	RR.	service businesses
BB.	labor-intensive businesses	SS.	socialism
CC.	macroeconomics	TT.	stakeholders
DD.	microeconomics	UU.	supply
EE.	monetary policy	VV.	supply curve

1. _____ Value of all the final goods and services produced by domestic businesses that includes receipts from overseas operations and excludes receipts from foreign-owned businesses within a nation's borders

2. _____ Buyers' willingness and ability to purchase products

3. _____ Use of government revenue collection and spending to influence the business cycle

4. _____ The study of how society uses scarce resources to produce and distribute goods and services

5. _____ The study of how consumers, businesses, and industries collectively determine the quantity of goods and services demanded and supplied at different prices

6. _____ Period during which income, employment, production, and spending rise

7. _____ The physical, human-made elements used to produce goods and services, such as factories and computers, can also refer to the funds that finance the operations of a business

8. _____ The conversion of public ownership to private ownership

9. _____ The combination of innovation, initiative, and willingness to take the risks required to create and operate new businesses

10. _____ Tendency of the world's economies to act as a single interdependent economy

11. _____ Statistics that measure variables in the economy

12. _____ Specific quantity of a product that the seller is able and willing to provide

13. _____ Situation in which so many buyers and sellers exist that no single buyer or seller can individually influence market prices

14. _____ Situation in which many sellers differentiate their products from those of competitors in at least some small way

15. _____ Rivalry among businesses for the same customer

16. _____ Point at which quantity supplied equals quantity demanded

17. _____ Period during which national income, employment, and production all fall

18. _____ The study of "big picture" issues in an economy, including competitive behavior among firms, the effect of government policies, and overall resource allocation issues

19. _____ Monthly statistic that measures changes in the prices of about 400 goods and services that consumers buy

20. _____ Money left over after expenses and taxes have been deducted from revenue generated by selling goods and services

21. _____ Means by which a society distributes its resources to satisfy its people's needs

22. _____ Market in which there are no direct competitors so that one company dominates

23. _____ Market dominated by a few producers

24. _____ Land, forests, minerals, water, and other tangible assets usable in their natural state

25. _____ Individuals or groups to whom business has a responsibility

26. _____ Graph of the quantities that sellers will offer for sale, regardless of demand, at various prices

27. _____ Graph of the quantities of product that buyers will purchase at various prices

28. _____ Government policy and actions taken by the Federal Reserve Board to regulate the nation's money supply

29. _____ Fluctuations in the rate of growth that an economy experiences over a period of several years

30. _____ Firms whose primary objective is something other than returning a profit to their owners

31. _____ Expertise gained through experience or association

32. _____ Economic system in which the government owns and operates all productive resources and determines all significant economic choices

33. _____ Economic system in which the government controls most of the factors of production and regulates their allocation

34. _____ Economic system in which decisions about what to produce and in what quantities are decided by the market's buyers and sellers

35. _____ Economic system characterized by public ownership and operation of key industries combined with private ownership and operation of less-vital industries

36. _____ Economic system based on economic freedom and competition

37. _____ Economic condition in which prices rise steadily throughout the economy

38. _____ Economic condition in which prices fall steadily throughout the economy

39. _____ Value of all the final goods and services produced by businesses located within a nation's borders; excludes receipts from overseas operations of domestic companies

40. _____ Businesses that require large investments in capital assets

41. _____ Businesses that produce tangible products

42. _____ Businesses that perform useful activities for customers

43. _____ Businesses in which labor costs are more significant than capital costs

44. _____ All the people who work for an organization

45. _____ Ability to perform in one or more ways that competitors cannot match

46. _____ A statistical measure of price trends at the producer and wholesaler levels

47. _____ A profit-seeking organization that provides goods and services that a society wants or needs

48. _____ A critical resource or capability a company must possess before it can enter a particular market or industry

Learning Objectives—Short Answer or Essay Questions

1. Define what a business is and identify four vital social and economic contributions that businesses make.

2. Differentiate between goods-producing and service businesses, and list five factors contributing to the increase in the number of service businesses.

3. Differentiate between a free-market system and a planned system.

4. Explain how supply and demand interact to affect price.

5. Discuss the four major economic roles of the U.S. government.

6. Explain how a free-market system monitors its economic performance.

7. Identify five challenges you will face as a business professional in the coming years.

Critical Thinking Questions

1. Describe Adam Smith's concept of capitalism and compare that to capitalism in the U.S. today.

2. Explain what a regulated industry is and briefly state the arguments for and against regulation.

3. How is the consumer price index (CPI) calculated and how is it used? Discuss some limitations of the CPI.

Exploring the Internet

Search the Internet to find the most recent annual report for a Fortune 500 company. (You can find a list of these companies at www.fortune500.com.) Relate what you find in this report to the five challenges you will face as a business professional in the coming years that are described in the text.

True-False—Answers

1. True	6. True	11. True
2. False	7. False	12. True
3. True	8. True	13. False
4. False	9. False	14. True
5. True	10. True	

Multiple Choice—Answers

1. D	6. B	11. C
2. B	7. B	12. A
3. D	8. A	13. A
4. A	9. D	14. D
5. C	10. C	

Match the Terms and Concepts with Their Definitions-Answers

1. X	17. PP	33. KK
2. L	18. DD	34. T
3. S	19. J	35. SS
4. P	20. NN	36. F
5. CC	21. O	37. Z
6. QQ	22. GG	38. K
7. D	23. JJ	39. W
8. LL	24. HH	40. E
9. Q	25. TT	41. V
10. U	26. VV	42. RR
11. N	27. M	43. BB
12. UU	28. EE	44. Y
13. OO	29. C	45. T
14. FF	30. II	46. MM
15. H	31. AA	47. B
16. R	32. G	48. A

Learning Objectives—Short Answer or Essay Questions - Answers

1. **Define what a business is, and identify four vital social and economic contributions that businesses make.**

A business is a profit-seeking activity that provides goods and services to satisfy consumers' needs. The driving force behind most businesses is the chance to earn a profit; however, nonprofit organizations exist to provide society with a social or educational service. Businesses make four vital contributions: They provide society with necessities; they provide people with jobs and a means to prosper; they pay taxes that are used by the government to provide services for its citizens; and they reinvest their profits in the economy, thereby increasing a nation's wealth.

2. **Differentiate between goods-producing and service businesses, and list five factors contributing to the increase in the number of service businesses.**

Goods-producing businesses produce tangible goods and tend to be capital intensive, whereas service businesses produce intangible goods and tend to be labor intensive. The number of service businesses is increasing because (1) consumers have more disposable income to spend on taking care of themselves; (2) many services target consumers' needs brought about by changing demographic patterns and lifestyle trends; (3) consumers need assistance with using and integrating new technology into their business operations and lifestyles; (4) companies are turning to consultants and other professionals for advice to remain competitive; and (5) in general, barriers to entry are lower for service companies than they are for goods-producing businesses.

3. **Differentiate between a free-market system and a planned system.**

In a free-market system, individuals have a high degree of freedom to decide what is produced, by whom, and for whom. Moreover, the pursuit of private gain is regarded as a worthwhile goal. In a planned system, governments limit the individual's freedom of choice in order to accomplish government goals, control the allocation of resources, and restrict private ownership to personal and household items. The pursuit of private gain is nonexistent under a planned system. Nearly all modern economies fall somewhere between purely free-market and purely planned.

4. **Explain how supply and demand interact to affect price.**

In the simplest sense, supply and demand affect price in the following manner: When the price goes up, the quantity demanded goes down but the supplier's incentive to produce more goes up. When the price goes down, the quantity demanded increases, whereas the quantity supplied may (or may not) decline. When the interests of buyers and sellers are in balance, an equilibrium price is established. However, adjusting price or supply to meet or spur demand does not guarantee profitability; business may not be able to adjust costs and price far enough and quickly enough. The important thing to remember is that in a free-market system, the interaction of supply and demand determines what is produced and in what amounts.

5. **Discuss the four major economic roles of the U.S. government.**

First, the U.S. government fosters competition by enacting laws and regulations, by enforcing antitrust legislation, and by approving mergers and acquisitions, with the power to block those that might restrain competition. Second, it regulates certain industries where competition would be wasteful or excessive. Third, it protects stakeholders from potentially harmful actions of businesses. Finally, it contributes to economic stability by regulating the money supply and by spending for the public good.

6. **Explain how a free-market system monitors its economic performance.**

Economists evaluate economic performance by monitoring a variety of economic indicators, such as unemployment statistics, housing starts, durable-goods orders, and inflation. They compute the consumer price index (CPI) to keep an eye on price changes—especially inflation. In addition, economists measure the productivity of a nation by computing the country's gross domestic product (GDP)—the sum of all goods and services produced by both domestic and foreign companies as long as they are located within a nation's boundaries.

7. **Identify five challenges that businesses are facing in the global economy.**

The five challenges identified in the chapter are (1) producing quality products and services that satisfy customers' changing needs, (2) thinking like an entrepreneur, even if you're an employee in a large company, (3) thinking globally and embracing a culturally diverse workforce, (4) behaving in an ethically and socially responsible manner, and (5) keeping pace with technology and electronic commerce.

Critical Thinking Questions - Answers

1. Describe Adam Smith's concept of capitalism and compare that to capitalism in the U.S. today.

According to Smith, in the ideal capitalist economy (pure capitalism), the market (an arrangement between buyer and seller to trade goods and services) serves as a self-correcting mechanism—an "invisible hand" to ensure the production of the goods that society wants in the quantities that society wants, without regulation of any kind.

Because he believed the market is its own regulator, Smith was opposed to government intervention. He held that if anyone's prices or wages strayed from acceptable levels set for everyone, the force of competition would drive them back. In modern practice, however, the government often intervenes in free-market systems to accomplish goals that leaders deem socially or economically desirable. This practice of limited intervention is characteristic of a mixed economy or mixed capitalism, which is the economic system of the United States and most other countries. For example, federal, state, and local governments intervene in the U.S. economy in a variety of ways, such as influencing particular allocations of resources through tax incentives, prohibiting or restricting the sale of certain goods and services, or setting price controls.

2. Explain what a regulated industry is and briefly state the arguments for and against regulation.

In a regulated industry, close government control is substituted for free competition, and competition is either limited or eliminated. In extreme cases, regulators may even decide who can enter an industry, what customers they must serve, and how much they can charge. For years, the telecommunications, airline, banking, and electric utility industries fell under strict government control. However, the trend over the past few decades has been to open up competition in regulated industries by removing or relaxing existing regulations. Hopes are that such deregulation will allow new industry competitors to enter the market, create more choices for customers, and keep prices in check. But the debate is ongoing about whether deregulation achieves these goals.

3. How is the consumer price index (CPI) calculated and how is it used? Discuss some limitations of the CPI.

The consumer price index (CPI) measures the rate of inflation by comparing the change in prices of a representative "basket" of consumer goods and services, such as clothing, food, housing, and utilities. A numerical weight is assigned to each item in the basket to adjust for each item's relative importance in the marketplace. The CPI has always been a hot topic because it is used by the government to index Social Security payments, and it is widely used by businesses in various contracts to calculate cost-of-living increases. However, like most economic indicators, the CPI is not perfect. Although it is based on data from thousands of retail establishments across the country, the representative basket of goods and services may not reflect the prices and consumption patterns of the area in which you live or of your specific household.

Exploring the Internet-Answers

Search the Internet to find the most recent annual report for a Fortune 500 company. (You can find a list of these companies at www.fortune500.com.) Relate what you find in this report to the five challenges you will face as a business professional in the coming years that are described in the text.

Your analysis should include information on how your chosen company goes about producing quality goods and services that satisfy customers' changing needs, in addition to how they incorporate entrepreneurial thinking into their business processes in order to foster innovation. Remember that this is important even though we are discussing a large company.

It is also essential to consider how this company is thinking globally and embracing a culturally diverse workforce and keeping pace with technology and electronic commerce to enable them to build a sustainable competitive advantage.

Finally, will your company's marketing, accounting, and financial practices along with its environmental performance stand up to the continued pressure from environmental groups, consumers, employees, and government regulators to act ethically and responsibly?

Chapter 2
Ethics and Corporate Social Responsibility

Learning Objectives
After reading this chapter, you should be able to:

1. Discuss what it means to practice good business ethics and highlight three factors that influence ethical behavior.
2. Identify three steps that businesses are taking to encourage ethical behavior and explain the advantages and disadvantages of whistle-blowing.
3. List four questions you might ask yourself when trying to make an ethical decision.
4. Explain the difference between an ethical dilemma and an ethical lapse.
5. Explain the controversy surrounding corporate social responsibility.
6. Discuss how businesses can become more socially responsible.
7. Define sustainable development and explain the strategic advantages of managing with sustainability as a priority.

True-False
Indicate whether the statement is generally true or false by placing a "T" or an "F" in the space provided. If it is a false statement, correct it so that it becomes a true statement.

_____ 1. The concept of corporate social responsibility (CSR) is that businesses have no obligation to society other than obeying the law and the pursuit of profits.

_____ 2. The application of moral standards to business situations is the basis for business ethics.

_____ 3. As headline-grabbing scandals have shown, most businesses are run by unethical managers who fail to make a positive contribution to their communities.

_____ 4. If a company is obeying the law that means that they are also behaving ethically.

_____ 5. The practice of hiring employees away from competitors for the purpose of acquiring trade secrets is generally seen as unethical.

_____ 6. Supplying stakeholders with enough information to make intelligent decisions about a company's products, people, and practices is a good rule of thumb for determining whether the company is operating with a sufficient level of transparency.

_____ 7. Executives and employees can avoid potential harm to stakeholders by the proper handling of company information.

_____ 8. Practices considered unethical in the United States are also considered unethical in the rest of the world.

_____ 9. Clear standards of behavior and a spirit of ethical awareness can be considered the foundation of an ethical business climate.

_____ 10. Behaving ethically can be one of the most effective tools for executives to inspire ethical behavior in their employees.

_____ 11. All ethical decisions will impact all stakeholder groups equally.

_____ 12. Business and society are at odds and one does not need the other in order to be healthy and productive.

_____ 13. The term *greenwashing* refers to the efforts of companies to claim social responsibility without actually taking steps to improve in that regard.

_____ 14. At the minimum, companies practicing corporate social responsibility (CSR) should take responsibility for the consequences of their actions and limit the negative impact of their operations.

_____ 15. Strategic CSR is the concept of aligning an organization's social contributions with their strategic goals.

_____ 16. Companies can produce and deliver products without generating pollution or consuming natural resources.

_____ 17. A sustainable operation will meet the needs of the present without compromising the ability of future generations to meet their own needs.

_____ 18. Consumerism and materialism are synonymous and refer to the conspicuous need of individuals to pursue wealth and luxury.

_____ 19. Public companies (companies that sell shares of their company to the public through the stock market) have no obligation to their investors.

_____ 20. As defined by the Americans with Disabilities Act, a disability refers only to physical handicaps.

Multiple Choice

Circle the best answer for each of the following questions.

1. It can be said that ethics are:
   a. Principles and standards of moral behavior
   b. Precisely the same from culture to culture
   c. Legally binding
   d. Both a and c

2. Which of the following is a way in which companies can contribute to society?
   a. By making useful products
   b. By providing employment
   c. By paying taxes
   d. All of the above

3. Which of the following is not a criterion for ethical business behavior?
   a. Obeying all laws and regulations
   b. Not causing harm to others
   c. Announcing ethical initiatives through advertising and public relations
   d. Competing fairly and honestly

4. Pretexting is the practice of:
   a. Sending important information to company stakeholders before releasing it to the media
   b. Lying about who you are in order to get information you couldn't get otherwise
   c. Managers reading employees' e-mail
   d. Hiring employees from competitors to gain trade secrets

5. Which of the following has the least influence on ethical business behavior?
   a. Cultural differences
   b. Local laws and regulations
   c. Knowledge
   d. Organizational behavior

6. Having discovered a potential ethical issue, a manager should:
   a. Attempt to resolve the issue in a timely and effective manner
   b. Save the company from embarrassment at all costs
   c. Take personal responsibility for this issue
   d. All of the above

7. For a company's code of ethics to be effective it should be supported by:
   a. A formal training program
   b. A system through which employees can get help with difficult ethical situations
   c. Employee commitment to following it
   d. All of the above

8. Utilitarianism is an ethical decision-making approach that seeks to:
   a. Maximize a company's profits and minimize losses
   b. Make the best use of a company's resources
   c. Put environmental concerns before all others
   d. Create the greatest good for the greatest number of people

9. An ethical dilemma is:
   a. A situation where an individual makes a decision that is clearly wrong
   b. The discovery of ethical wrongdoing by a coworker
   c. A situation in which one must choose between two conflicting but arguably valid sides
   d. None of the above

10. Which of the following perspectives on CSR is considered dishonest and, therefore, unethical?
    a. Minimalist
    b. Defensive
    c. Cynical
    d. Conscientious

11. Which of the following statements is most correct?
    a. Strategic CSR involves the donation of money, employees' time, or other resources
    b. Strategic CSR involves social contributions that are directly aligned with the company's overall business strategy
    c. Philanthropy involves social contributions that are directly aligned with the company's overall business strategy
    d. Strategic CSR and philanthropy are essentially the same

12. Taking a sustainable, long-term view of how a company impacts the environment and stakeholders around the world may not:
    a. Ensure short-term success
    b. Ensure continued availability of resources
    c. Better prepare the organization for changes in government regulations and social expectations
    d. Signal that the organization is well managed

13. The Equal Employment Opportunity commission was created under which piece of government legislation?
    a. Americans with Disabilities Act
    b. Civil Rights Act of 1964
    c. Occupational Safety and Health Act of 1970
    d. The Equal Rights Amendment

Match the Terms and Concepts with Their Definitions

A. affirmative action
B. code of ethics
C. conflict of interest
D. consumerism
E. corporate social responsibility (CSR)
F. discrimination
G. ecology
H. ethical dilemma
I. ethical lapse
J. ethics
K. green marketing
L. global warming

M. identity theft
N. insider trading
O. justice
P. nongovernmental organizations (NGO)
Q. philanthropy
R. social audit
S. strategic CSR
T. sustainable development
U. transparency
V. utilitarianism
W. whistle-blowing

1. _____ Activities undertaken by businesses to recruit and promote members of groups whose economic progress had been hindered through either legal barriers or established practices

2. _____ Study of the relationships among living things in the water, air, and soil, their environments, and the nutrients that support them

3. _____ Nonprofit groups that provide charitable services or promote social and environmental causes

4. _____ A decision-making approach that seeks to create the greatest good for the greatest number of people affected by the decisions

5. _____ The idea that business has obligations to society beyond the pursuit of profits

6. _____ The degree to which affected parties can observe relevant aspects of transactions or decisions

7. _____ The resolution of ethical questions and other dilemmas in a manner that is consistent with generally accepted standards of right and wrong

8. _____ The donation of money, time, goods, or services to charitable, humanitarian, or educational institutions

9. _____ Operating business in a manner that minimizes pollution and resource depletion, ensuring that future generations will have vital resources

10. _____ In a social and economic sense, denial of opportunities to individuals on the basis of some characteristic that has no bearing on their ability to perform in a job

11. _____ Written statement setting forth the principles that guide an organization's decisions

12. _____ Situation in which both sides of an issue can be supported with valid arguments

13. _____ Crimes in which thieves steal personal information and use it to take out loans and commit other types of fraud

14. _____ The disclosure of information by a company insider that exposes illegal or unethical behavior by others within the organization

15. _____ Assessment of a company's performance in the area of social responsibility

16. _____ The use of unpublicized information that an individual gains from the course of his or her job to benefit from fluctuations in the stock market

17. _____ The rules or standards governing the conduct of a person or group

18. _____ Movement that pressures businesses to consider consumer needs and interests

19. _____ Efforts by companies to distinguish themselves by practicing sustainable development and communicating these efforts to consumers

20. _____ Situation in which a business decision may be influenced by the potential for personal gain

21. _____ Situation in which an individual or group makes a decision that is morally wrong, illegal, or unethical

22. _____ Social contributions that are directly aligned with a company's overall business strategy

23. _____ A gradual rise in average temperatures around the planet; caused by increases in carbon dioxide emissions

Learning Objectives—Short Answer or Essay Questions

1. Discuss what it means to practice good business ethics, and highlight three factors that influence ethical behavior.

2. Identify three steps that businesses are taking to encourage ethical behavior, and explain the advantages and disadvantages of whistle-blowing.

3. List four questions you might ask yourself when trying to make an ethical decision.

4. Explain the difference between an ethical dilemma and an ethical lapse.

5. Explain the controversy surrounding corporate social responsibility.

6. Discuss how businesses can become more socially responsible.

7. Define sustainable development and explain the strategic advantages of managing with sustainability as a priority.

Critical Thinking Questions

1. As a company's senior manager, you've discovered that one of your foreign distributors has regularly been paying government officials a "handling fee" in order to ensure that shipments of your product make it to your customers in his country in a timely fashion. This distributor does not work directly for your company and is one of the biggest sellers of your product in the world. In addition, your international legal department tells you that they can find no law prohibiting this payment in the distributor's country. Explain how you would proceed with your relationship with this distributor and how you came to this decision.

2. As the leader of a corporation, explain the steps you can take to create and sustain an ethical business.

3. Explain the various positive impacts that strategic CSR can make to benefit business and society simultaneously.

Exploring the Internet

Search the Internet to find a code of ethics published by a corporation or trade association. Will this code of ethics elicit ethical behavior in those toward whom the code is directed? Why do you believe it will or will not be effective?

True-False—Answers

		7.	True	14.	True
1.	False	8.	False	15.	True
2.	True	9.	True	16.	False
3.	False	10.	True	17.	True
4.	False	11.	False	18.	False
5.	True	12.	False	19.	False
6.	True	13.	True	20.	False

Multiple Choice—Answers

1.	A	6.	A	11.	B
2.	D	7.	D	12.	A
3.	C	8.	D	13.	B
4.	B	9.	C		
5.	B	10.	C		

Match the Terms and Concepts with Their Definitions

1.	A	9.	T	17.	J
2.	G	10.	F	18.	D
3.	P	11.	B	19.	K
4.	V	12.	H	20.	C
5.	E	13.	M	21.	I
6.	U	14.	W	22.	S
7.	O	15.	R	23.	L
8.	Q	16.	N		

Learning Objectives—Short Answer or Essay Questions—Answers

1. **Discuss what it means to practice good business ethics and highlight three factors that influence ethical behavior.**

   For people in business to actively practice ethical behavior, they must obey all laws and regulations, in addition to competing fairly and honestly, communicating truthfully, and not causing harm to others.

   The three factors that appear to have the most impact on ethical behavior are:
   - *Cultural differences*- What may be considered unethical in the United States may be an accepted practice in another culture. Managers may need to consider a wide range of issues, including acceptable working conditions, minimum wage levels, product safety issues, and environmental protection.
   - *Knowledge*- The more you know and the better you understand a situation, the better your chances are of making an ethical decision.
   - *Organizational behavior*- Organizations that strongly enforce company codes of conduct and provide ethics training help employees recognize and reason through ethical problems. Similarly, companies with strong ethical practices set a good example for employees.

2. **Identify three steps that businesses are taking to encourage ethical behavior and explain the advantages and disadvantages of whistle-blowing.**

   To help avoid ethical breaches, organizations are creating a written code of ethics that defines the values and principles that should be used to guide decisions in conjunction with enhanced employee communications efforts, a formal training program, asking for employee commitment to following it, and the implementation of a system through which employees can get help with ethically difficult situations.

   Whistle-blowing is an employee's disclosure to the media or government authorities of illegal, unethical, or harmful practices by the company. An environment that supports whistle-blowing can discourage unethical behavior from ever happening, or stop it before it has the opportunity to grow into a larger problem. Whistle-blowing can bring high costs: Public accusation of wrongdoing hurts the business's reputation, requires attention from managers who must investigate the accusations, and damages employee morale. Moreover, whistle-blowers risk being fired or demoted, and they often suffer career setbacks, financial strain, and emotional stress. The fear of such negative repercussions may allow unethical or illegal practices to go unreported.

3. **List four questions you might ask yourself when trying to make an ethical decision.**

   - Is the decision legal? (Does it break any laws?)

   - Is it balanced? (Is it fair to all concerned?)

- Can you live with it? (Does it make you feel good about yourself?)

- Is it feasible? (Will it actually work in the real world?)

4. Explain the difference between an ethical dilemma and an ethical lapse.

An ethical dilemma is a situation in which one must choose between two conflicting but arguably valid sides. All ethical dilemmas have a common theme: the conflict between the rights of two or more important groups of people. The second type of situation is an ethical lapse, in which an individual makes a decision that is clearly wrong, such as divulging trade secrets to a competitor.

5. Explain the controversy surrounding corporate social responsibility.

While the cynical perspective of CSR can be dismissed simply because it is dishonest and therefore unethical, the overall debate is less clear. Some proponents of the minimalist view equate CSR with *collectivism*, a term that suggests communism and socialism. Some consider CSR demands from NGOs and other outsiders to be little more than extortion "fundamentally antagonistic to capitalist enterprise." At the other extreme, some critics of contemporary business seem convinced that corporations can never be trusted and that every CSR initiative is a cynical publicity stunt.

6. Discuss how businesses can become more socially responsible.

A two-tiered approach to CSR can yield a practical, ethical answer to this complex dilemma. At the first tier, companies must take responsibility for the consequences of their actions and limit the negative impact of their operations. This can be summarized as "do no harm," and it is not a matter of choice. Just as it has a right to expect certain behavior from all citizens, society has a right to expect a basic level of responsible behavior from business, including minimizing pollution and waste, minimizing the depletion of natural resources, being honest with all stakeholders, offering real value in exchange for prices asked, and avoiding exploitation of employees, customers, suppliers, communities, and investors.

At the second tier, moving beyond "do no harm" does become a matter of choice. Companies can choose to help in whatever way investors, managers, and employee see fit, but the choices are a matter of free will.

7. Define sustainable development and explain the strategic advantages of managing with sustainability as a priority.

Sustainable development is defined by the United Nations as development that "meets the needs of the present without compromising the ability of future generations to meet their own needs." Businesses that recognize the link between environmental performance and sustained financial well-being are discovering that spending now to prevent pollution can end up saving more money down the road (by reducing cleanup costs, litigation expenses, and production costs). Besides addressing ethical and financial concerns, such efforts can help companies build goodwill with customers, communities, and other stakeholders. In addition to better stewardship of shared natural resources, sustainable development is also a smart business strategy. By taking a broad and long-term view of their companies' impact on the environment and stakeholders throughout the world, managers can ensure the continued availability of the resources their organizations need and be better prepared for changes in government regulations and shifting social expectations. In fact, some experts believe sustainability is a good measure of the quality of management in a corporation.

Critical Thinking Questions—Answers

1. **As a company's senior manager, you've discovered that one of your foreign distributors has regularly been paying government officials a "handling fee" in order to ensure that shipments or your product make it to your customers in his country in a timely fashion. This distributor does not work directly for your company and is one of the biggest sellers of your product in the world. In addition, your international legal department tells you that they can find no law prohibiting this payment in the distributor's country. Explain how you would proceed with your relationship with this distributor and how you came to this decision.**

While it is likely that no laws are being broken, this is still a sticky ethical situation. From the perspective of utilitarianism, continuing the relationship with this distributor seems like the right thing to do because the most people benefit from this decision. Benefits include revenue for the company, jobs for the company's employees, revenue for the distributor, and access to the product for the distributor's customers. Even considering the four ethical decision-making questions could guide the company to deciding to continue this relationship. After all, it seems balanced in that all parties are willing to supply or buy the product under these circumstances, and it is clearly feasible. The rub is in the other two questions, especially "Does it feel right?" In American and most Western cultures, paying a government official a special fee seems like political corruption despite the fact that the activity may be common in other countries and cultures. This sort of activity, from an American perspective, also hints at the possibility of the existence of other activities that might be less ethical and even illegal in the distributor's country. Clearly, this is a tough decision to make, and there may be no right answer. The best answer for this company, however, would be to ask the distributor to discontinue these practices or risk termination of this business relationship.

2. **As the leader of a corporation, explain the steps you can take to create and sustain an ethical business.**

   - *Lead by example.* Nothing is more important than demonstrating your commitment to ethics than behaving ethically yourself.
   - *Don't tolerate unethical behavior.* At the same time, you have to show that bad decisions won't be accepted. Let one go without correction, and you'll probably see another one before long.
   - *Inspire concretely.* Tell employees how they will personally benefit from participating in

ethics initiatives. People respond better to personal benefits than to company benefits.

- *Acknowledge reality.* Admit errors. Discuss what went right, what went wrong, and how the company can learn from the mistakes. Solicit employee opinion and act on those opinions. If you only pretend to be interested, you'll make matters worse.
- *Communicate, communicate, communicate.* Ethics needs to be a continuous conversation, not a special topic brought up only in training sessions or when a crisis hits.
- *Be honest.* Tell employees what you know as well as what you don't know. Talk openly about ethical concerns and be willing to accept negative feedback.
- *Hire good people.* If you hire good people (not people who are good at their jobs, but people who are good, period) and create an ethical environment for them, you'll get ethical behavior. If you hire people who lack good moral character, you're inviting ethical lapses, no matter how many rules you write.

3. **Explain how strategic CSR differs from general philanthropy or the defensive perspective of business versus society.**

Strategic CSR makes more sense than general philanthropy or an antagonistic business-versus-society mindset, for several reasons. First, because business and society are mutually dependent, choices that weaken one or the other will ultimately weaken both. Second, investments that benefit the company are more likely to be sustained over time. Third, making sizable investments in a few strategically focused areas, rather than spreading smaller amounts of money around through generic philanthropy, will yield greater benefits to society.

Exploring the Internet—Answer

Search the Internet to find a code of ethics published by a corporation or trade association. Will this code of ethics elicit ethical behavior in those toward whom the code is directed? Why do you believe it will or will not be effective?

A code of ethics will be effective if it clearly defines the values and principles that should be used to guide decisions for any stakeholder in this business. Also, to be truly effective, a code must be supported by employee communications efforts, a formal training program, employee commitment to following it, and a system through which employees can get help with ethically difficult situations. (Your explanation should discuss how well the code defines these values and principles and how well the company supports the code by its other action.)

Chapter 3
The Global Marketplace

Learning Objectives
After reading this chapter, you should be able to:

1. Discuss why nations trade.
2. Explain why nations restrict international trade and list four forms of trade restrictions.
3. Highlight three protectionist tactics nations use to give their domestic industries a competitive edge.
4. Explain how trading blocs affect trade.
5. Highlight the opportunities and challenges of conducting business in other countries.
6. List five ways to improve communication in an international business relationship.
7. Identify five forms of international business activity.
8. Discuss terrorism's impact on globalization.

True-False
Indicate whether the statement is generally true or false by placing a "T" or an "F" in the space provided. If it is a false statement, correct it so that it becomes a true statement.

1. _____ Most industrialized nations have the resources and capabilities to produce everything their citizens want or need at prices they are willing to pay.

2. _____ Many companies need to find international markets because their ambitions are too large to be realized within their home countries.

3. _____ Virtually no country has an absolute advantage in any industry; instead it may have a comparative advantage.

4. _____ The United States imports more goods than it exports, but it exports more services than it imports.

5. _____ A quota is an extreme type of an embargo which is a complete ban on the import or export of certain products or even all trade between certain countries.

6. _____ Rather than restrict imports, some countries subsidize domestic producers so that their prices can compete favorably in the global marketplace.

7. _____ Across the EU, trade now flows among member countries in much the same way as it does among states in the United States.

8. _____ The euro has been adopted as the standard currency by all of the EU member nations.

9. _____ A weak dollar means that relative to most currencies around the world, the U.S. dollar buys more units of those other currencies than it has in the recent past.

10. _____ When communicating with businesspeople from another country or culture, it is best to insist that they adapt to your communication style and customs.

11. _____ All U.S. companies are bound by the Foreign Corrupt Practices Act (FCPA), which outlaws payments with the intent of getting government officials to break the laws of their own countries.

12. _____ A joint venture is a special type of strategic alliance in which two or more firms join together to create a new business entity that is legally separate and distinct from its parents.

Multiple Choice
Circle the best answer for each of the following questions.

1. Companies engage in international trade to achieve which of the following?
   a. To benefit from economies of scale
   b. To give consumers more options
   c. To create more revenue for governments
   d. All of the above

2. Comparative advantage theory suggests:
   a. International trade creates an unfair advantage for some countries
   b. The globalization of the marketplace puts small companies at a disadvantage
   c. Each country should specialize in those areas where it can produce more efficiently than other countries
   d. None of the above

3. The total value of a country's exports minus the total value of its imports, over some period of time, determines its:
   a. Balance of payments
   b. Balance of power
   c. Exchange rate
   d. Balance of trade

4. The concept of fair trade suggests:
    a. Countries don't take artificial steps to minimize their own weakness and blunt the advantage of other countries
    b. Buyers voluntarily agree to pay more than the prevailing market price in order to help producers earn a living wage, enough money to satisfy their essential needs
    c. Companies from all countries should obey the same rules
    d. None of the above

5. Which of the following is not a type of trade restriction?
    a. Tariffs
    b. Quotas
    c. GATT
    d. Embargoes

6. Which of the following organizations would not be considered a trading bloc?
    a. WTO
    b. NAFTA
    c. EU
    d. APEC

7. A benefit of the dollar being strong relative to other currencies is:
    a. U.S. products are more price competitive in foreign markets
    b. U.S. buyers pay less for imported goods
    c. U.S. firms are under less price pressure from imports in the U.S. market
    d. Overseas tourists are encouraged to visit the U.S.

8. When a government implements a currency devaluation it:
    a. Lowers the value of its currency relative to other currencies
    b. May be attempting to boost the country's economy by making its products and services more affordable in foreign markets
    c. May be attempting to protect domestic companies by increasing the price of imports
    d. All of the above

9. Ethnocentrism is:
    a. Assigning a wide range of generalized (and often superficial or even false) attributes to an individual on the basis of membership in a particular culture or social group without considering the individual's unique characteristics
    b. The preference to work with people from your own cultural or ethnic group
    c. The tendency to judge all other groups according to your own group's standards, behaviors, and customs
    d. None of the above

10. In a common-law legal system:
    a. Tradition, custom, and judicial interpretation play important roles
    b. Legal parameters are specified in detailed legal codes only
    c. Religious principles dictate legal decisions
    d. None of the above

11. Which of the following is a type of strategic alliance?
    a. Importing and exporting
    b. Foreign direct investment (FDI)
    c. Licensing
    d. Joint venture

12. Which of the following aspects of business has not been affected by the rise in global terrorism?
    a. Transportation
    b. Staffing
    c. Banking
    d. None of the above

Match the Terms and Concepts with Their Definitions

A. absolute advantage
B. balance of payments
C. balance of trade
D. comparative advantage theory
E. devaluation
F. dumping
G. economies of scale
H. embargo
I. ethnocentrism
J. euro
K. exchange rate
L. exporting
M. foreign direct investment (FDI)
N. fair trade

O. free trade
P. importing
Q. joint venture
R. licensing
S. multinational corporations (MNCs)
T. protectionism
U. quotas
V. stereotyping
W. strategic alliance
X. tariffs
Y. trade deficit
Z. trade surplus
AA. trading blocs

1. _____ Savings from buying parts and materials, manufacturing, or marketing in large quantities

2. _____ A nation's ability to produce a particular product with fewer resources per unit of output than any other nation

3. _____ Theory that states that a country should produce and sell to other countries those items it produces most efficiently

4. _____ Total value of the products a nation exports minus the total value of the products it imports, over some period of time

5. _____ Favorable trade balance created when a country exports more than it imports

6. _____ Government policies aimed at shielding a country's industries from foreign competition

7. _____ Sum of all payments one nation receives from other nations minus the sum of all payments it makes to other nations, over some specified period of time

8. _____ International trade unencumbered by restrictive measures

9. _____ Rate at which the money of one country is traded for the money of another

10. _____ Taxes levied on imports

11. _____ Limits placed on the quantity of imports a nation will allow for a specific product

12. _____ Total ban on trade with a particular nation (a sanction) or of a particular product

13. _____ Charging less than the actual cost or less than the home-country price for goods sold in other countries

14. _____ Organizations of nations that remove barriers to trade among their members and that establish uniform barriers to trade with nonmember nations

15. _____ A unified currency used by roughly half the nations in the European Union

16. _____ A voluntary approach to trading with artisans and farmers in developing countries, guaranteeing them above-market prices as a way to protect them from exploitation by larger, more-powerful trading partners

17. _____ A move by one government to drop the value of its currency relative to the value of other currencies

18. _____ Assigning a wide range of generalized attributes, which are often superficial or even false, to an individual based on his or membership in a particular culture or social group

19. _____ Judging all other groups according to your own group's standards, behaviors, and customs.

20. _____ Purchasing goods or services from another country and bringing them into one's own country

21. _____ Selling and shipping goods or services to another country

22. _____ Agreement to produce and market another company's product in exchange for a royalty or fee

23. _____ Long-term relationship in which two or more companies share ideas, resources, and technologies in order to establish competitive advantages

24. _____ Cooperative partnership in which organizations share investment costs, risks, management, and profits in the development, production, or selling of products

25. _____ Investment of money by foreign companies in domestic business enterprises

26. _____ Companies with operations in more than one country

27. _____ Unfavorable trade balance created when a country imports more than it exports

Learning Objectives—Short Answer or Essay Questions

1. Discuss why nations trade.

2. Explain why nations restrict international trade, and list four forms of trade restrictions.

3. Highlight three protectionist tactics nations use to give their domestic industries a competitive edge.

4. Explain how trading blocs affect trade.

5. Highlight the opportunities and challenges of conducting business in other countries.

6. List five ways to improve communication in an international business relationship.

7. Identify five forms of international business activity.

8. Discuss terrorism's impact on globalization.

Critical Thinking Questions

1. Explain the comparative advantage theory and relate it to a U.S. industry that is familiar to you.

2. Discuss the arguments for and against free trade.

3. Explain why it is easier for some products to find global markets than it is for others.

Exploring the Internet

Explore the World Trade Organization's website at www.wto.org and then explore the Global Exchange website's critical position of the WTO at www.globalexchange.org/wto. Discuss the differing perspective of the two organizations and briefly explain where you stand on the issue of free trade and why.

True-False - Answers

1. False	5. False	9. False
2. True	6. True	10. False
3. True	7. True	11. True
4. True	8. False	12. True

Multiple Choice - Answers

1. A	5. C	9. C
2. C	6. A	10. A
3. D	7. B	11. D
4. B	8. D	12. D

Match the Terms and Concepts with Their Definitions - Answers

1. G	10. X	19. I
2. A	11. U	20. P
3. D	12. H	21. L
4. C	13. F	22. R
5. Z	14. AA	23. W
6. T	15. J	24. Q
7. B	16. N	25. M
8. O	17. E	26. S
9. K	18. V	27. Y

Learning Objectives—Short Answer or Essay Questions - Answers

1. **Discuss why nations trade.**

   Nations trade to obtain raw materials and goods that are unavailable to them or too costly to produce. International trade benefits nations by increasing a country's total output, offering lower prices and greater variety to its consumers, subjecting domestic oligopolies and monopolies to competition, and allowing companies to expand their markets and achieve production and distribution efficiencies.

2. **Explain why nations restrict international trade, and list four forms of trade restrictions.**

   Nations restrict international trade to boost local economies, to shield domestic industries from head-to-head competition with overseas rivals, to save specific jobs, to give weak or new industries a chance to grow strong, and to protect a nation's security. The four most commonly used forms of trade restrictions are tariffs (taxes, surcharges, or duties levied against imported goods), quotas (limitations on the amount of a particular good that can be imported), embargoes (the banning of imports and exports of certain goods), and sanctions (politically motivated embargoes).

3. **Highlight three protectionist tactics that nations use to give their domestic industries a competitive edge.**

   From time to time countries give their domestic producers a competitive edge by imposing restrictive import standards, such as requiring special licenses or unusually high product standards, by subsidizing certain domestic producers so they can compete more favorably in the global marketplace, and by dumping or selling large quantities of a product at a lower price than it costs to produce the good or at a lower price than the good is sold for in its home market.

4. Explain how trading blocs affect trade.

Trading blocs are regional groupings of countries within which trade barriers have been removed. These alliances ease trade among bloc members and strengthen barriers for nonmembers. Critics of trading blocs fear that as members become more protective of their regions, those not in the bloc could suffer. Proponents see them as a way to help smaller or younger nations compete with producers in more-developed nations. The four most powerful trading blocs today are the Association of Southeast Asian Nations (ASEAN), the Mercosur, the North American Free Trade Agreement (NAFTA), and the European Union (EU).

5. Highlight the opportunities and challenges of conducting business in other countries.

Conducting business in other countries can provide such opportunities as increased sales, operational efficiencies, exposure to new technologies, and consumer choices. At the same time, it poses challenges such as the need to learn unique laws, customs, and ethical standards. Furthermore, it exposes companies to the risks of political and economic instabilities, volatile currencies, international trade relationships, and the threat of global terrorism.

6. List five ways to improve communication in an international business relationship.

To improve international communication, learn as much as you can about the culture and customs of the people you are working with; keep an open mind and avoid stereotyping; anticipate misunderstandings and guard against them by clarifying your intent; adapt your style to match the style of others; and learn how to show respect in other cultures.

7. Identify five forms of international business activity.

Importing and exporting, licensing, franchising, strategic alliances and joint ventures, and foreign direct investment are five of the most common forms of international business activity. Each provides a company with varying degrees of control and entails different levels of risk and financial commitment.

8. Discuss terrorism's impact on globalization.

Terrorism could prompt companies to withdraw from the global marketplace and focus more on doing business within their national borders. But the likelihood of moving in that direction is remote. Most multinational organizations have too much at stake to move backward; they see globalization as the key to their future. Global terrorism, however, does pose new challenges to world trade. Tighter security, border-crossing delays, cargo restrictions, and higher transportation costs are having an impact on the free flow of goods in the global marketplace. These obstacles are forcing some companies to rethink their inventory and manufacturing strategies.

Critical Thinking Questions - Answers

1. **Explain the comparative advantage theory and relate it to a U.S. industry that is familiar to you.**

   The comparative advantage theory suggests that each country should specialize in those areas where it can produce more efficiently than other countries, and it should trade for goods and services that it can't produce as economically. The basic argument behind the comparative advantage theory is that such specialization and exchange will increase a country's total output and allow both trading partners to enjoy a higher standard of living.

   Comparative advantage is both relative and dynamic. In other words, no matter how good you are, you only have an advantage if you are better than someone else, and no advantage is preordained to last forever. For example, the U.S. auto industry was once the unquestioned world leader, but over the course of just a couple of decades, Japan was able to reduce that advantage with quality products at lower prices, and Toyota is now the world's largest auto company. South Korea is repeating the Japanese strategy with its own brands, most notably Hyundai. The United States remains one of the world's most competitive countries, to be sure, but dozens of other countries now compete for the same employees, customers, and investments.

2. **Discuss the arguments for and against free trade.**

   Trade that takes place without these interferences is known as free trade. Free trade is not a universally welcomed concept, in spite of the positive connotation of the word "free." Supporters claim it is the best way to ensure prosperity for everyone, but detractors call it unfair to too many people and a threat to the middle class. In addition, some critics argue that free trade makes it too easy for companies to exploit workers around the world by pitting them against one another in a "race to the bottom," in which production moves to whichever country has the lowest wages and fewest restrictions regarding worker safety and environmental protection. This complaint has been at the heart of recent protests over free trade and globalization in general. However, this criticism is rebutted by some researchers who say that companies prefer to do business in countries with stable, democratic governments. Consequently, says this camp, less-developed nations are motivated to improve their economic and social policies.

   One common example of the criticism of free trade involves the negotiating advantages that large international companies can have when buying from small farmers and other producers in multiple countries. The result, it is argued, is that prices get pushed so low that those producers struggle to earn enough money to survive because somebody, somewhere, is always willing to work for less or sell for less. One response to this situation is the concept of fair trade, in which buyers voluntarily agree to pay more than the prevailing market price in order to help producers earn a living wage, enough money to satisfy their essential needs.

3. Explain why it is easier for some products to find global markets than it is for others.

Some industries, such as consumer electronics and apparel, are highly globalized. These products are easy to make just about anywhere, and they don't cost much to ship. Others, including products that are expensive to ship relative to their sales value (such as steel) are less globalized. Services are among the least-globalized product categories, given the obvious costs and difficulties of delivering most services at long distances.

Exploring the Internet - Answers

Explore the World Trade Organization's website at <u>www.wto.org</u> and then explore the Global Exchange website's critical position of the WTO at <u>www.globalexchange.org/wto</u> . Discuss the differing perspective of the two organizations and briefly explain where you stand on the issue of free trade and why.

The WTO positions itself as a permanent forum for negotiating, implementing, and monitoring international trade procedures and for mediating trade disputes among its roughly 150 member countries. The organization's primary goal is to improve the welfare of people worldwide by helping international trade function more efficiently.

Global Exchange claims the WTO is the most powerful legislative and judicial body in the world. By promoting the "free trade" agenda of multinational corporations above the interests of local communities, working families, and the environment, the WTO has systematically undermined democracy around the world.

WTO says these criticisms are unjustified and based on misunderstandings of what the WTO does. You should explain why this difference in perception exists and where you feel the reality of the situation lies.

Chapter 4
Business Systems

Learning Objectives
After reading this chapter, you should be able to:

1. Identify eight principles of systems thinking that can improve your skills as a manager.
2. Describe the value chain and value web concepts.
3. Define supply chain management and explain its strategic importance.
4. Highlight the differences between quality control and quality assurance.
5. Identify four major ways that businesses use information.
6. Differentiate between operational information systems and professional and managerial systems, and give several examples of each.
7. Identify seven important information systems issues that managers must be aware of in today's business environment.

True-False
Indicate whether the statement is generally true or false by placing a "T" or an "F" in the space provided. If it is a false statement, correct it so that it becomes a true statement.

1. _____A system is an interconnected and coordinated set of elements and processes that converts inputs to desired outputs.

2. _____ Principles of systems thinking show people how they contribute to the overall goal of an organization and help ensure that the entire system works efficiently.

3. _____The production system is a company's plan to generate sales revenue and earn a profit based on that revenue, represents the firm's highest-level system, and defines the major elements that make the company what it is—and is not.

4. _____According to Professor Michael Porter, many companies have come to realize that doing everything themselves is always the most efficient way to run a business.

5. _____Offshoring, a variation on outsourcing, can shift jobs to either another company or to an overseas division of the same company.

6. _____Traditional economic theory suggests that outsourcing lower-level jobs to countries with lower wages is good for U.S. companies.

7. _____ The best supply chains function to serve the company without regard for the company's customers or vendors.

8. _____ The value chain is the part of the overall supply chain that acquires and manages the goods and services needed to produce whatever it is the company produces, and then deliver it to the final customer.

9. _____ The only benefit of a well-designed facility comes from helping companies operate more productively by reducing wasted time and wasted materials.

10. _____ The term *capacity* refers to the volume of manufacturing or service capability that an organization can handle.

11. _____ When an airline offers hundreds of opportunities for passengers to fly from Dallas to Chicago every day, and every customer on these flights gets the same service at the same time, the providing of this service can be considered mass production.

12. _____ The majority of workers in the United States are now involved in the farming and manufacturing business sectors.

13. _____ Even when production quantities are very high, monitoring a sample is not enough to provide a reasonable estimate of the quality of the entire process.

14. _____ Production control systems are used to manage the production of goods and services by controlling production lines, robots, and other machinery and equipment.

15. _____ Office automation systems capture, organize, and capitalize on all the interactions that a company has with its customers, from marketing surveys and advertising through sales orders and customer support.

16. _____ It can be said that information technology is a paradox, in which tools designed to save time can waste as much time as they save.

17. _____ The total cost of ownership (TCO) of IT systems, which includes the purchase costs of hardware, software, and networking plus expenses for installation, customization, training, upgrades, and maintenance, can be three to five times higher than the purchase price.

Multiple Choice
Circle the best answer for each of the following questions.

1. Technology companies failed after the demise of the dot-com boom because of which of the following reasons?
    a. Misjudging how hard it would be to build repeatable and measurable traffic levels
    b. How expensive it was to build and maintain websites that large numbers of visitors would want to visit regularly
    c. How reluctant many major companies were to shift their advertising budgets from proven media such as magazines and television to the then-unproven medium of the Internet
    d. All of the above

2. Traditional economic theory suggests that outsourcing lower-level jobs to countries with lower wages is good for U.S. companies because:
   a. It frees up money and employees to work on more valuable activities
   b. It helps raise the standard of living in other countries and thereby expands opportunities for U.S. companies to export their products
   c. Both a and b
   d. None of the above

3. Supply chain management (SCM) combines business procedures and policies with computer systems that integrate which elements of the supply chain into a cohesive system?
   a. Outside suppliers, internal company processes, and customers
   b. Employees, customers, and stockholders
   c. Management, labor unions, and vendors
   d. None of the above

4. Which of the following is not a benefit of SCM to managers?
   a. SCM can help companies manage the complex risks involved in a supply chain
   b. SCM can coordinate the numerous relationships in the supply chain and help managers focus their attention on the most important company-to-company relationships
   c. SCM can help companies manage uncooperative vendors and customers by making them align with the company's SCM protocol
   d. SCM helps balance the competing interests of the various functional areas and both capacity and capability along the entire chain

5. Which of the following is not a SCM issue?
   a. Inventory control
   b. Corporate communications
   c. Purchasing
   d. Logistics (getting materials and products from place to place)

6. Which of the following planning systems and techniques has the largest scope within an organization?
   a. CRM
   b. ERP
   c. MRP
   d. MRP II

7. When choosing the location of production facilities, a manager must consider such factors as:
   a. land, construction, labor costs
   b. local taxes and local living standards
   c. transportation for both raw materials and finished products
   d. All of the above

8. Which of the following is not a benefit of using PERT?
   a. It helps managers identify the optimal sequencing of activities
   b. It helps managers identify the expected time for project completion
   c. It helps managers to see how finished products will look and operate before physical prototypes are built
   d. It helps managers identify the best use of resources within a complex project

9. Productivity is:
   a. The efficiency with which a company can convert inputs to outputs
   b. The value of the outputs divided by the value of the inputs
   c. Neither
   d. Both

10. Which of the following is not a way in which services differ from goods?
    a. Services can be produced and stored for future use
    b. Customers are often involved in—and can affect the quality of—the service delivery
    c. Many services are consumed at the same time they are produced
    d. Customers often dictate when and where services are performed

11. Total quality management (TQM):
    a. Is both a management philosophy and a strategic management process
    b. Is a statistical application designed to eliminate defects to less than 3.4 defects per million opportunities
    c. Focuses on delivering the optimal level of quality to customers by building quality into every organizational activity
    d. Both a and c

12. The acronym DMAIC is short for:
    a. Design, Manufacture, Analyze, Implement, Correct
    b. Define, Measure, Analyze, Improve, Control
    c. Design, Measure, Analyze, Import, Combine
    d. Define, Manufacture, Analyze, Implement, Complete

13. ISO 9000 and ISO 14000 are quality standards that focus on:
    a. The actual quality of goods and services
    b. Customer satisfaction
    c. The processes and policies that companies use to create their goods and services
    d. Consumer safety

14. A company's chief information officer (CIO) is expected to deliver quality information, which can be defined as all of the following except:
    a. Explicable (everyone in the organization should be able to understand it)
    b. Relevant (the information delivered to each person relates directly to his or her needs)
    c. Accurate (it is both current and free from errors)
    d. Timely (delivered in time to make a difference)

15. This type of system assists managers in solving highly unstructured and nonroutine problems through the use of models and specialized databases:
    a. MIS
    b. DSS
    c. CRM
    d. TPS

16. Which of the following is not a type of malicious software?
    a. Worms
    b. Trojan horses
    c. Cookies
    d. Spyware

17. Firewalls are:
    a. Devices for monitoring internal e-mail
    b. Social networking sites
    c. Portable storage devices
    d. Hardware or software devices that block access to intruders

Match the Terms and Concepts with Their Definitions

A.	artificial intelligence	J.	databases
B.	business model	K.	electronic business (e-business)
C.	capacity planning	L.	enterprise resource planning (ERP)
D.	chief information officer (CIO)	M.	Gantt chart
E.	core competencies	N.	information
F.	critical path	O.	information systems (IS)
G.	customized production	P.	information technology (IT)
H.	data	Q.	insight
I.	data mining	R.	intellectual property

S.   inventory
T.   inventory control
U.   just-in-time (JIT)
V.   lean systems
W.   malware
X.   management information system
     (MIS)
Y.   manufacturing resource planning
     (MRP II)
Z.   mass customization
AA. mass production
BB. material requirements planning (MRP)
CC. outsourcing
DD. production
EE. production and operations
     management
FF. production forecasts
GG. productivity

HH. program evaluation and review
     technique (PERT)
II.   purchasing
JJ. quality assurance
KK. quality control
LL. Six Sigma
MM. statistical process control (SPC)
NN. statistical quality control (SQC)
OO. supply chain
PP. supply chain management (SCM)
QQ. system
RR. total quality management (TQM)
SS. value chain
TT. value webs
UU. viruses

1. _____An interconnected and coordinated set of elements and processes that converts
        inputs to desired outputs

2. _____A company's plan to generate sales revenue and earn a profit based on that
        revenue

3. _____The creation of goods and services

4. _____All the elements and processes that add value as raw materials are transformed
        into the final products made available to the ultimate customer

5. _____Functions in which a company has a distinct advantage over its competitors

6. _____Contracting out certain business functions or operations to other companies

7. _____Multidimensional networks of suppliers and outsourcing partners

8. _____A set of connected systems that coordinates the flow of goods and materials
        from suppliers all the way through to final customers

9. _____Estimates of future demand for a company's products

10. _____Goods and materials kept in stock for production or sale

11. _____A generally accepted synonym for information systems; many companies use
        IT to refer to the department that manages information systems

12. _____ The acquisition of the raw materials, parts, components, supplies, and finished products required to produce goods and services

13. _____ Computer system that helps manufacturers get the correct materials where they are needed, when they are needed, without unnecessary stockpiling

14. _____ An expansion of MRP that links to a company's financial systems and other processes

15. _____ Materials and resource planning systems that encompass the entire organization

16. _____ Overseeing all the activities involved in producing goods and services

17. _____ The business procedures, policies, and computer systems that integrate the various elements of the supply chain into a cohesive system

18. _____ Establish the overall level of resources needed to meet customer demand

19. _____ A type of bar chart used for project or process scheduling

20. _____ A planning tool that managers of complex projects use to determine the optimal order of activities, the expected time for project completion, and the best use of resources

21. _____ In a PERT network diagram, the sequence of operations that requires the longest time to complete

22. _____ The efficiency with which an organization can convert inputs to outputs

23. _____ Manufacturing systems that maximize productivity by reducing waste and delays

24. _____ Inventory management in which goods and materials are delivered throughout the production process right before they are needed

25. _____ The creation of identical goods or services, usually in large quantities

26. _____ The creation of a unique good or service for each customer

27. _____ Manufacturing approach in which part of the product is mass produced and the remaining features are customized for each buyer

28. _____ Creative outputs with commercial value, such as design ideas, manufacturing processes, brands, and chemical formulas

29. _____ A more comprehensive approach of companywide policies, practices, and procedures to ensure that every product meets quality standards

30. _____ Invasive programs that reproduce by infecting legitimate programs

31. _____ Use of random sampling and control charts to monitor the production process

32. _____ A management philosophy and strategic management process that focuses on delivering the optimal level of quality to customers by building quality into every organizational activity

33. _____ A quality management program that strives to eliminate deviations between the actual and desired performance of a business system

34. _____ Facts, numbers, statistics, and other individual bits and pieces that by themselves do not necessarily constitute useful information

35. _____ Useful knowledge, often extracted from data

36. _____ A deep level of understanding about a particular subject or situation

37. _____ Computerized files that collect, sort, and cross-reference data

38. _____ A method of extracting previously unknown relationships among individual data points in a database

39. _____ A high-level executive responsible for understanding the company's information needs and creating systems and procedures to deliver that information to the right people at the right time

40. _____ A collective label for all technologies and processes used to manage business information

41. _____ Determine the right quantities of supplies and products to have on hand and tracking where those items are

42. _____ Computer system that provides managers with information and support for making routine decisions

43. _____ Ability of computers to solve problems through reasoning and learning and to simulate human sensory perceptions

44. _____ Organization in which all major business functions take full advantage of the capabilities and efficiencies of information technology

45. _____ Short for malicious software; computer programs that are designed to disrupt

websites, destroy information, or enable criminal activity

46. _____ Monitoring all aspects of the production process to see whether the process is operating as it should

47. _____ Measuring quality against established standards after the good or service has been produced and weeding out any defective products

Learning Objectives—Short Answer or Essay Questions

1. Identify nine principles of systems thinking that can improve your skills as a manager.

2. Describe the value chain and value web concepts.

3. Define supply chain management and explain its strategic importance.

4. Highlight the differences between quality control and quality assurance.

5. Identify four major ways that businesses use information.

6. Differentiate between operational information systems and professional and managerial systems, and give several examples of each.

7. Identify seven important information systems issues that managers must be aware of in today's business environment.

Critical Thinking Questions

1. Supply chain management (SCM) can have a profound impact on the success of a company if implemented well. Discuss some situations in which you think SCM might not work.

2. Discuss the differences between mass production and mass customization, and cite a few examples of products or services that might fall into either category.

3. Discuss how businesses can turn information into a competitive advantage.

Exploring the Internet

1. Search "digital rights management" on popular business websites like www.businessweek.com and www.wsj.com and explore some of the articles that you find. Use this information as the basis for discussion of how digital rights management affects consumers and producers of popular music.

True-False - Answers

1.	True	7.	False	13.	False
2.	True	8.	False	14.	True
3.	False	9.	True	15.	False
4.	False	10.	True	16.	True
5.	True	11.	True	17.	True
6.	True	12.	False		

Multiple Choice - Answers

1.	D	7.	D	13.	C
2.	C	8.	C	14.	A
3.	A	9.	D	15.	B
4.	C	10.	A	16.	C
5.	B	11.	D	17.	D
6.	B	12.	B		

Match the Terms and Concepts with Their Definitions - Answers

1.	QQ	11.	P	21.	F
2.	B	12.	II	22.	GG
3.	DD	13.	BB	23.	V
4.	SS	14.	Y	24.	U
5.	E	15.	L	25.	AA
6.	CC	16.	EE	26.	G
7.	TT	17.	PP	27.	Z
8.	OO	18.	C	28.	R
9.	FF	19.	M	29.	JJ
10.	S	20.	HH	30.	UU

31. MM	37. J	43. A
32. RR	38. I	44. K
33. LL	39. D	45. W
34. H	40. O	46. NN
35. N	41. T	47. KK
36. Q	42. X	

Learning Objectives—Short Answer or Essay Questions - Answers

1. **Identify eight principles of systems thinking that can improve your skills as a manager.**

   The eight principles identified in the chapter are (1) helping everyone see the big picture, including how individual employees and departments contribute to the company's overall goals; (2) understanding how individual systems really work and how they interact so that any changes you make are helpful rather than harmful; (3) understanding problems before you try to fix them, thereby avoiding the temptation of the quick-fix solution that only causes more problems in the long run; (4) understanding the potential impact of solutions before you implement them in order to avoid unintended consequences; (5) avoiding the temptation to just move problems from one subsystem to the next without fixing them; (6) avoiding the "bigger hammer" syndrome, in which you keep applying an inappropriate solution with ever-increasing energy; (7) understanding how feedback works in a system so that you can improve each process by learning from experience; and (8) using mistakes as opportunities to learn and improve.

2. **Describe the value chain and value web concepts.**

   The value chain is a helpful way to view all the elements and processes that add value as raw materials are transformed into the final products made available to the ultimate customer. The linear value chain concept tends to make the most sense when companies do most or all of the major business functions themselves. As more and more companies rely on business partners and outsourcing relationships, the multidimensional value web has become a more realistic model for many.

3. **Define supply chain management, and explain its strategic importance.**

   Supply chain management (SCM) combines business procedures and policies with computer systems that integrate the various elements of the supply chain into a cohesive system, encompassing all the company's outside suppliers and distribution partners. SCM continues to grow in strategic importance because it helps firms manage risks, manage relationships, and manage the many trade-offs that must be made in the supply chain.

4. **Highlight the differences between quality control and quality assurance.**

   Quality control involves measuring product quality against established standards *after* the good or service has been produced, and weeding out any defects. Quality assurance takes a more comprehensive and proactive approach with companywide policies, practices, and procedures to ensure quality is built into products from the beginning.

5. **Identify four major ways that businesses use information.**

   Businesses use information in every decision and every facet of operations, but the four areas highlighted in the chapter are research and development (from understanding customer needs to developing new products), planning and control (assembling plans, then monitoring how well the business executes them), marketing and sales (connecting with customers), and communication and collaboration (sharing information and working together throughout the organization).

6. **Differentiate between operational information systems and professional and managerial systems, and give several examples of each.**

   Operational systems collect and process the data and information that represent the daily business of the enterprise, from sales receipts to production data to accounting records. The most common types are transaction processing systems, process and production control systems, office automation systems, and customer relationship management systems. In contrast, professional and managerial systems assist with analysis and decision making in both the professional and managerial ranks of the organization. Among the many varieties of these systems are knowledge management systems, management information systems, decision support systems, and executive support systems.

7. **Identify seven important information systems issues that managers must be aware of in today's business environment.**

   Managers in virtually all industries need to address these seven technology-related challenges: ensuring privacy and security, protecting property rights, guarding against information overload, monitoring productivity, managing total cost of ownership, helping employees develop the necessary technical skills, and maintaining the human touch in interactions with both employees and customers.

Critical Thinking Questions - Answers

1. **Supply chain management (SCM) can have a profound impact on the success of a company if implemented well. Discuss some situations in which you think SCM might not work.**

   Since SCM success stems from managing risk, relationships, and trade-offs with supply chain partners, any situation where the partners might be at a disadvantage will decrease the chance of SCM initiatives being productive because the partners will be less willing to cooperate for concern of self-protection. Also, in situations where the company starting the SCM initiative has proven unreliable to its partners—

for example, consistently delivering late to customers or not paying vendors on time—SCM efforts may be doomed to failure.

2. **Discuss the differences between mass production and mass customization, and cite a few examples of products or services that might fall into either category.**

Both goods and services can be created through mass production, or mass customization, depending on the nature of the product and the desires of target customers. In mass production, identical goods or services are created, usually in large quantities, such as when Apple churns out a million identical iPhones or American Airlines offers hundreds of opportunities for passengers to fly from Dallas to Chicago every day. Mass production has the advantage of economies of scale, but it can't deliver many of the unique goods and services that today's customers demand. On the other hand, fully customized production can offer uniqueness, but usually at a much higher price. An attractive compromise in many cases is mass customization, in which part of the product is mass produced, then the remaining features are customized for each buyer. Carvin guitars are examples of mass-customized products, as is your local ice cream shop that will make a frozen treat to your order.

3. **Discuss how businesses can turn information into a competitive advantage.**

The first step in turning information into a competitive advantage is understanding the difference between data (recorded facts and statistics), information (useful knowledge, often extracted from data), and insight (a deep level of understanding about a particular situation). The transformation from data to insight requires a combination of technology, information-management strategies, creative thinking, and business experience—and companies that excel at this transformation have a huge advantage over their competitors. In fact, entire industries can be created when a single person looks at the same data and information everyone else is looking at but sees things in a new way, yielding insights that no one has ever had before.

Exploring the Internet - Answers

1. **Search "digital rights management" on popular business websites like www.businessweek.com and www.wsj.com and explore some of the articles that you find. Use this information as the basis for discussion of how digital rights management (DRM) affects consumers and producers of popular music.**

You will find articles on how DRM helps to protect the artists of popular music and those that produce and sell the music either on CD or in a downloadable format. This protection comes primarily in helping to ensure that those who have rights to the music get paid by people interested in owning a copy of a given song or other recorded work. You will also notice that there are DRM issues concerning the format in which these recordings are issued. For example, in many cases MP3 files cannot be played on iPods, and music purchased through iTunes cannot be played on non-Apple devices. Your discussion should consider the rights of the consumer and the originators of these recordings, and form some opinion on how the industry should proceed in order to treat all parties equitably.

Chapter 5
Business Structures

Learning Objectives
After reading this chapter, you should be able to:

1. List five advantages and four disadvantages of sole proprietorships.
2. List five advantages and two disadvantages of partnerships.
3. Explain the differences between common and preferred stock from a shareholder's perspective.
4. Highlight the advantages and disadvantages of public stock ownership.
5. Cite four advantages and three disadvantages of corporations.
6. Delineate the three groups that govern a corporation and describe the role of each.
7. Identify six main synergies companies hope to achieve by combining their operations.

True-False
Indicate whether the statement is generally true or false by placing a "T" or an "F" in the space provided. If it is a false statement, correct it so that it becomes a true statement.

1. _____ The three most common forms of business ownership are sole proprietorships, trusts, and corporations.

2. _____ In a general partnership all general partners have unlimited liability.

3. _____ The law generally treats the corporation the same way it treats an individual person.

4. _____ Common stockholders have the right of first claim on the corporation's assets after all the company's debts have been paid.

5. _____ The primary reason for taking a company public is to help finance the enterprise.

6. _____ S corporations are taxed twice, as they must pay tax on the company's profits, and individual shareholders must pay income taxes on their share of the company's profits received as dividends.

7. _____ A subsidiary corporation is a special type of parent company that owns other companies for investment reasons.

8. _____ The board of directors in a corporation is responsible for declaring dividends,

guiding corporate affairs, reviewing long-term strategic plans, selecting corporate officers, and overseeing financial performance.

9. _____ A hostile takeover occurs when one or more individuals purchase a company's publicly traded stock by using borrowed funds.

10. _____ A company's culture is a general term that describes the way people in a given organization approach the day-to-day business of running a company.

11. _____ A joint venture is a type of strategic alliance where companies jointly develop, produce, or sell products through the formation of a separate legal entity.

Multiple Choice
Circle the best answer for each of the following questions.

1. Selecting a form of business ownership structure involves which of the following?
   a. Knowing your long-term goals and how you plan to achieve them
   b. Your desire for ownership
   c. Your tolerance for risk
   d. All of the above

2. Which of the following is not an advantage of a sole proprietorship?
   a. Ease of establishment
   b. You enjoy limited personal liability
   c. Company profits do not get taxed twice
   d. You don't have to reveal your performance or plans to anyone

3. Which of the following is not true about a limited partnership?
   a. All partners are considered equal by law, and all are liable for the business's debts
   b. One or more persons act as general partners who run the business
   c. Non-general partners are passive investors
   d. For limited partners their liability (the amount of money they can lose) is limited to the amount of their capital contribution

4. Which of the following is not true about a corporation?
   a. It can receive, own, and transfer property
   b. It can make contracts
   c. It can transfer profits to owners untaxed
   d. It can sue and be sued

5. Which of the following type of corporations trades its shares on a stock exchange?
   a. A private corporation
   b. A public corporation
   c. A closed corporation
   d. A closely held corporation

6. Which of the following is not an advantage of taking a company public?
   a. Establishment of an independent market value for the company
   b. Reduced administrative and legal demands
   c. Enhanced visibility for the company
   d. Increased liquidity of the company's stock

7. Which of the following is not a criterion for a corporation to receive S status?
   a. It must have more than 75 investors
   b. None of the investors may be nonresident aliens
   c. The company must be a domestic (U.S.) corporation
   d. The company can issue only one class of common stock

8. Which of the following is true about a limited liability company (LLC)?
   a. The number of shareholders is restricted
   b. It has the tax advantages of a partnership
   c. It has the personal liability protection of a corporation
   d. Both b and c

9. Which type of corporation is not incorporated in the United States?
   a. A foreign corporation
   b. An alien corporation
   c. A domestic corporation
   d. Both a and b

10. Which "c-level" executive is responsible for establishing company policies, managing corporate direction, and making the big decisions that will affect the company's growth and competitive position?
    a. CTO
    b. CIO
    c. CEO
    d. COO

11. Which of the following would not be considered an institutional investor?
    a. A wealthy individual
    b. A pension fund
    c. A religious organization
    d. A mutual fund

12. Which of the following statements best describes a consolidation?
    a. Two companies join to form a single entity
    b. Two companies create a new, third entity that then purchases the two original companies
    c. One company simply buys a controlling interest in the voting stock of another company
    d. An investor tries to convince enough shareholders to go against management and vote to sell

13. Which term means a company is purchasing a complementary company at a different level in the value chain?
    a. A horizontal merger
    b. A leveraged buyout
    c. A conglomerate merger
    d. A vertical merger

14. Which of the following is not a potential advantage of a merger or acquisition?
    a. Increase buying power as a result of larger size
    b. Increase revenue by cross-selling products to each other's customers
    c. Increase market share by combining product lines to provide more comprehensive offerings
    d. All of the above

15. Which acquisition defense tactic is simply a requirement that stockholders representing a large majority of shares approve any takeover attempt?
    a. A proxy fight
    b. The poison pill
    c. Shark repellent
    d. The white knight

Match the Terms and Concepts with Their Definitions

A. acquisition
B. board of directors
C. chief executive officer (CEO)
D. common stock
E. consolidation
F. corporation
G. dividends
H. general partnership
I. holding company
J. hostile takeover
K. leveraged buyout (LBO)
L. limited liability companies (LLCs)
M. limited partnership
N. liquidity

O. merger
P. parent company
Q. partnership
R. preferred stock
S. private corporation
T. proxy
U. public corporation
V. S corporation
W. shareholder activism
X. shareholders
Y. sole proprietorship
Z. stock certificate
AA. subsidiary corporations
BB. unlimited liability

1. _____Business owned by a single individual

2. _____Legal condition under which any damages or debts attributable to the business can also be attached to the owner because the two have no separate legal existence

59

3. _____Unincorporated business owned and operated by two or more persons under a voluntary legal association

4. _____Partnership in which all partners have the right to participate as co-owners and are individually liable for the business's debts

5. _____Partnership composed of one or more general partners and one or more partners whose liability is usually limited to the amount of their capital investment

6. _____Legally chartered enterprise having most of the legal rights of a person, including the right to conduct business, to own and sell property, to borrow money, and to sue or be sued; owners of the corporation enjoy limited liability

7. _____Owners of a corporation

8. _____Document that proves stock ownership

9. _____Shares whose owners have voting rights and have the last claim on distributed profits and assets

10. _____Distributions of corporate assets to shareholders in the form of cash or other assets

11. _____Shares that give their owners first claim on a company's dividends and assets after paying all debts

12. _____ Situation in which individuals or groups of investors purchase companies primarily with debt secured by the company's assets

13. _____Corporation that actively sells stock on the open market

14. _____The level of ease with which an asset can be converted to cash

15. _____Corporation with no more than 75 shareholders that may be taxed as a partnership; also known as a subchapter S corporation

16. _____Organizations that combine the benefits of S corporations and limited partnerships without the drawbacks of either

17. _____Corporations whose stock is owned entirely or almost entirely by another corporation

18. _____Company that owns most, if not all, of another company's stock and that takes an active part in managing that other company

19. _____ Company that owns most, if not all, of another company's stock but does not actively participate in the management of that other company

20. _____ In a broad sense, describes the policies, procedures, relationships, and systems in place to oversee the successful and legal operation of the enterprise; in a narrow sense, describes the responsibilities and performance of the board of directors

21. _____ Person appointed by a corporation's board of directors to carry out the board's policies and supervise the activities of the corporation

22. _____ Document authorizing another person to vote on behalf of a shareholder in a corporation

23. _____ Advocacy by individual or institutional shareholders, using their status as shareholders to influence management policies and decisions

24. _____ Group of people, elected by the shareholders, who have the ultimate authority in guiding the affairs of a corporation

25. _____ Combination of two companies in which one company purchases the other and assumes control of its property and liabilities

26. _____ Combination of two or more companies in which the old companies cease to exist and a new enterprise is created

27. _____ Form of business combination in which one company buys another company's voting stock

28. _____ Situations in which an outside party buys enough stock in a corporation to take control against the wishes of the board of directors and corporate officers

29. _____ Company owned by private individuals or companies

Learning Objectives—Short Answer or Essay Questions

1. List five advantages and four disadvantages of sole proprietorships.

2. List five advantages and two disadvantages of partnerships.

3. Explain the differences between common and preferred stock from a shareholder's perspective.

4. Highlight the advantages and disadvantages of public stock ownership.

5. Cite four advantages and three disadvantages of corporations.

6. Delineate the three groups that govern a corporation and describe the role of each.

7. Identify six main synergies companies hope to achieve by combining their operations.

Critical Thinking Questions

1. Discuss the two major issues that business owners need to consider when selecting a form of ownership.

2. Discuss the composition, roles, and responsibilities of a corporate board of directors.

3. Discuss the advantages and disadvantages of mergers and acquisitions (M&A).

True-False - Answers

1. False	5. True	9. False
2. True	6. False	10. True
3. True	7. False	11. True
4. False	8. True	

Multiple Choice - Answers

1. D	6. B	11. A
2. B	7. A	12. B
3. A	8. D	13. D
4. C	9. B	14. D
5. B	10. C	15. C

Match the Terms and Concepts with Their Definitions - Answers

1.	Y	11.	R	21.	C
2.	BB	12.	K	22.	T
3.	Q	13.	U	23.	W
4.	H	14.	N	24.	B
5.	M	15.	V	25.	O
6.	F	16.	M	26.	E
7.	X	17.	AA	27.	A
8.	Z	18.	P	28.	J
9.	D	19.	I	29.	S
10.	G	20.	CC		

Learning Objectives—Short Answer or Essay Questions - Answers

1. **List five advantages and four disadvantages of sole proprietorships.**

    Sole proprietorships have five advantages: (1) They are easy to establish, (2) they provide the owner with control and independence, (3) the owner reaps all the profits, (4) profits are taxed at individual rates, and (5) the company's plans and financial performance remain private. The four main disadvantages of a sole proprietorship are (1) the company's financial resources are usually limited, (2) management talent may be thin, (3) the owner is liable for the debts and damages incurred by the business, and (4) the business may cease when the owner dies.

2. **List five advantages and two disadvantages of partnerships.**

    In addition to being easy to establish and having profits taxed at individual rates, partnerships offer a greater ability to obtain financing, longevity, and a broader base of skills. The two main disadvantages of partnerships are unlimited liability for general partners and the potential for personality and authority conflicts.

3. **Explain the differences between common and preferred stock from a shareholder's perspective.**

    Common shareholders can vote and can share in the company's profits through discretionary dividends and adjustments in the market value of their stock. In other words, they can profit from their investment if the value of the stock rises above the price they paid for it, or they can lose money if the value of the stock falls below the price they paid for it. In contrast, preferred shareholders cannot vote, but they can get a fixed return (dividend) on their investment and a priority claim on assets after creditors.

4. **Highlight the advantages and disadvantages of public stock ownership.**

    Public stock ownership offers a company increased liquidity, enhanced visibility, financial flexibility, and an independently established market value for the stock. The disadvantages of public stock ownership are high costs, burdensome filing requirements, loss of ownership control, heightened public exposure, and loss of direct control over the market value of the company's stock.

5. **Cite four advantages and three disadvantages of corporations.**

    Because corporations are a separate legal entity, they have the power to raise large sums of capital, they offer the shareholders protection from liability, they provide liquidity for investors, and they have an unlimited life span. In exchange for these advantages, businesses pay large fees to incorporate, and they are taxed twice on company profits—corporations pay tax on profits and individuals pay tax on dividends (distributed corporate profits). Finally, if publicly owned, corporations must adhere to strict government reporting requirements.

6. Delineate the three groups that govern a corporation and describe the role of each.

Shareholders are the basis of the corporate structure. They elect the board of directors, who in turn hire the officers of the corporation. The corporate officers carry out the policies and decisions of the board. In practice, the shareholders and board members have often followed the lead of the chief executive officer.

7. Identify six main synergies companies hope to achieve by combining their operations.

By combining their operations, companies hope to eliminate redundant costs, increase their buying power, increase their revenue, improve their market share, eliminate manufacturing overcapacity, and gain access to new expertise and personnel.

Critical Thinking Questions - Answers

1. Discuss the major issues that business owners need to consider when selecting a form of ownership.

Taxes, liability, and ability to sell shares for the purpose of raising capital are the major issues in deciding what form a company should take. Certain forms, such as a sole proprietorship, are attractive from a tax standpoint in that the owner only needs to pay tax on profits once, but carry a reasonable amount of risk in that the owner is personally liable for the debts and actions of the company. Corporations, on the other hand, offer limited liability for the owners, but profits are taxed twice: once as a corporate tax and again when they are paid out as dividends to shareholders. Corporations also have the ability to sell shares to the public in order to raise funds, while sole proprietorships cannot. Other forms such as partnerships, LLCs and S corps are somewhere in the middle and offer different degrees of tax burden, liability limits, and fundraising ability.

2. Discuss the composition, roles, and responsibilities of a corporate board of directors.

The board of directors in a corporation represents the shareholders and is responsible for declaring dividends, guiding corporate affairs, reviewing long-term strategic plans, selecting corporate officers, and overseeing financial performance. Depending on the size of the company, the board might have anywhere from 3 to 35 directors, although 15 to 25 is the typical range for traditional corporations and perhaps 5 to 10 for smaller or newer corporations. Directors are usually paid a combination of an annual fee and stock options, and the right to buy company shares at a specified price.

The board's actual involvement in running the business varies from one company to another, from passive boards that contribute little to the management of the organization to extremely involved boards that participate in strategic decision making.

3. **Discuss the advantages and disadvantages of mergers and acquisitions (M&A).**

Companies pursue mergers and acquisitions for a wide variety of reasons: They might hope to reduce costs by eliminating redundant resources; increase their buying power as a result of their larger size; increase revenue by cross-selling products to each other's customers; increase market share by combining product lines to provide more comprehensive offerings; eliminate overcapacity; or gain access to new expertise, systems, and teams of employees who already know how to work together. Bringing a company under new ownership can also be an opportunity to replace or improve inept management and thereby help a company improve its performance.
Often these advantages are grouped under umbrella terms such as economies of scale, efficiencies, or synergies, which generally mean that the benefits of working together will be greater than if each company continued to operate independently.

While the advantages can be compelling, joining two companies is a complex process because it involves virtually every aspect of both organizations. For instance, executives have to agree on how the combination will be financed and how the power will be transferred and shared. Marketing departments need to figure out how to blend advertising campaigns and sales forces. Incompatible information systems often need to be rebuilt or replaced in order to operate together seamlessly. Companies often must deal with layoffs, transfers, and changes in job titles and work assignments. And through it all, the enterprise needs to keep its eye on customer service, accounting, and every other function.

Chapter 6
Small Business and Entrepreneurship

Learning Objectives
After reading this chapter, you should be able to:

1. Highlight the major contributions small businesses make to the U.S. economy.
2. Identify the key characteristics (other than size) that differentiate small businesses from larger ones.
3. Discuss three factors contributing to the increase in the number of small businesses.
4. Cite the key characteristics common to most entrepreneurs.
5. List three ways of going into business for yourself.
6. Identify six sources of small-business assistance.
7. Discuss the principal sources of small-business private financing.

True-False
Indicate whether the statement is generally true or false by placing a "T" or an "F" in the space provided. If it is a false statement, correct it so that it becomes a true statement.

_____ 1. The overwhelming majority of small businesses have no employees at all.

_____ 2. Business startups drop off sharply when the economy sours.

_____ 3. Sometimes the greatest service a business plan can provide an entrepreneur is the realization that "the concept just won't work."

_____ 4. A company's mission explains its purpose and what it hopes to accomplish.

_____ 5. Design and development plans provide information on the facilities, equipment, and labor needed.

_____ 6. In a franchise the franchisor (the small-business owner who contracts to sell the goods or services) pays the franchisee (the supplier) an initial startup fee then monthly royalties based on sale volume.

_____ 7. Growing too quickly is a significant source of business failures.

_____ 8. There are major differences between business incubators and business accelerators.

_____ 9. Angel investors are private individuals who put their own money into startups with the goal of eventually selling their interest for a large profit.

_____ 10. Credit cards are a safe way to finance a new business.

_____ 11. Initial roll out (IRO) is when a corporation offers its shares of ownership to the public for the first time.

Multiple Choice
Circle the best answer for each of the following questions.

1. According to the U.S. Small Business Administration (SBA) a small business is one that:
   a. Is independently owned and operated and is not dominant in its field
   b. Must have less than 25 employees
   c. Must make less than $5 million per year in revenue
   d. All of the above

2. All of the following are true about small businesses except:
   a. They employ about half of the private-sector workforce in the U.S.
   b. They create more than two-thirds of new jobs in the U.S.
   c. They tend to be risk adverse
   d. If U.S. small businesses were a separate country, they would constitute the third-largest economy in the world

3. Small companies tend to differ from large enterprises in which of the following ways?
   a. Most small firms have a narrower focus
   b. Most small businesses get by with limited resources
   c. They have more freedom to innovate and move quickly
   d. All of the above

4. A factor not contributing to the increase in the number of small businesses today is:
   a. The advent of e-commerce and other technological advances
   b. The growing diversity in entrepreneurship
   c. An increase in venture capital available
   d. Corporate downsizing and outsourcing

5. All of the following are characteristics of successful entrepreneurs except:
   a. They have a high degree of confidence
   b. They have significant financial resources
   c. They are driven by a passion to succeed
   d. They learn from their mistakes

6. Preparing a business plan serves which important functions?
    a. It guides the company operations and strategy for turning an idea into reality
    b. It ensures the entrepreneur that the business idea will work regardless of any obstacles
    c. It persuades lenders and investors to finance your business
    d. Both a and c

7. Which of the following is not an advantage of buying an existing business?
    a. The employees will be happy and the equipment will be functioning
    b. There is an established customer base
    c. There are functioning business systems in place
    d. The product or service is proven

8. Which of the following best describes a business format franchise?
    a. It grants the right to sell trademarked goods, which are purchased from the franchisor and resold
    b. It grants the right to open a business using a franchisor's name and format for doing business
    c. It grants the right to produce and distribute the manufacturer's products, using supplies purchased from the franchisor
    d. None of the above

9. Which of the following is not an advantage of purchasing a franchise?
    a. Instant name recognition
    b. A proven formula for success
    c. The freedom of franchisees to make their own decisions
    d. Standardized quality of goods and services

10. When small businesses fail, it is often for which one of the following reasons?
    a. Lack of management skills and experience
    b. Growing too fast
    c. Inadequate financing
    d. All of the above

11. Which of the following is a not a type of private financing?
    a. Credit cards
    b. Venture capitalists
    c. Selling shares of company on a stock exchange
    d. Borrowing money from a bank

12. Which if the following is true about venture capitalists?
    a. They only supply money to companies that they invest in
    b. They demand a small percentage of ownership in the companies they invest in
    c. They provide management expertise to the companies they invest in
    d. Both a and b

Match the Terms and Concepts with Their Definitions

A. business accelerators
B. business incubators
C. business plan
D. franchise
E. franchisee

F. franchisor
G. initial public offering (IPO)
H. small business
I. start-up companies
J. venture capitalists (VCs)

1. _____ Company that is independently owned and operated, is not dominant in its field, and meets certain criteria for the number of employees or annual sales revenue

2. _____ A written document that provides an orderly statement of a company's goals and a plan for achieving those goals

3. _____ New business ventures

4. _____ Business arrangement in which one business obtains rights to sell the goods or services of the supplier

5. _____ A corporation's first offering of shares to the public

6. _____ Supplier that grants a franchise to an individual or group (franchisee) in exchange for payments

7. _____ Facilities that house small businesses and provide support services during the company's early growth phases

8. _____ Similar in concept to incubators but focused more on advisory services and (in some cases) financing

9. _____ Investors who provide money to finance new businesses or turnarounds in exchange for a portion of ownership, with the objective of reselling the business at a profit

10. _____ Small-business owner who contracts for the right to sell goods or services of the supplier in exchange for some payment

Learning Objectives—Short Answer or Essay Questions

1. Highlight the major contributions small businesses make to the U.S. economy.

2. Identify the key characteristics (other than size) that differentiate small businesses from larger ones.

3. Discuss three factors contributing to the increase in the number of small businesses.

4. Cite the key characteristics common to most entrepreneurs.

5. List three ways of going into business for yourself.

6. Identify six sources of small-business assistance.

7. Discuss the principle sources of small-business private financing.

Critical Thinking Questions

1. Describe how some of today's well-known entrepreneurs have used some of the twelve characteristics of successful entrepreneurs described in the book to make their companies successful.

2. Discuss the pros and cons of buying a franchise.

Exploring the Internet

Go to www.bplans.com and click on the "Browse free sample plans" link. Select one of the plans and briefly discuss how the business in question communicates the following. Also include your thoughts on how the author of this plan could have improved the effectiveness of this plan.

- *Mission and objectives*
- *Company and industry*
- *Products or services*
- *Market and competition*
- *Management*
- *Marketing strategy*
- *Design and development plans*

- *Operations plan*
- *Overall schedule*
- *Critical risks and problems*
- *Financial projections and requirements*
- *Exit strategy*

True-False - Answers

1. True	5. False	9. True
2. False	6. False	10. False
3. True	7. True	11. False
4. True	8. False	

Multiple Choice - Answers

1. A	5. B	9. C
2. C	6. D	10. D
3. D	7. A	11. C
4. C	8. B	12. C

Match the Terms and Concepts with Their Definitions – Answers

1. H	5. G	9. J
2. C	6. F	10. E
3. I	7. B	
4. D	8. A	

Learning Objectives—Short Answer or Essay Question - Answers

1. **Highlight the major contributions small businesses make to the U.S. economy.**

   Small businesses bring new ideas, processes, and vigor to the marketplace. They generate about half of private sector output and create between two-thirds and three-quarters of all new jobs. Small businesses introduce new goods and services, provide specialized products, and supply the needs of large corporations. Additionally, they spend almost as much as big businesses in the economy each year.

2. **Identify the key characteristics (other than size) that differentiate small businesses from larger ones.**

   In general, small businesses tend to sell fewer products and services to a more targeted group of customers. They have closer contact with their customers and many tend to be more open-minded and innovative because they have less to lose than established companies. Small-business owners generally make decisions faster and give employees more opportunities for individual expression and authority. Because they have limited resources, however, small-business owners often must work harder and perform a variety of job functions.

3. **Discuss three factors contributing to the increase in the number of small businesses.**

   One factor is the advancement of e-commerce and other technologies, which make it easier to start a small business, compete with larger firms, or work from home. A second factor is the increase in the number of women and minorities who are interested in becoming entrepreneurs. Third, corporate downsizing and outsourcing have pushed more professionals into self-employment and created more markets for their goods and services.

4. **Cite the key characteristics common to most entrepreneurs.**

   Successful entrepreneurs are highly disciplined, intuitive, innovative, ambitious individuals who are eager to learn and like to set trends. They prefer excitement and are willing to take risks to reap the rewards. Few start businesses for the sole purpose of making money.

5. **List three ways of going into business for yourself.**

   You can start a new company from scratch, you can buy an existing company, or you can invest in a franchise. Each option has its advantages and disadvantages when it comes to cost, control, certainty, support, and independence.

6. Identify six sources of small-business assistance.

First, government agencies and nonprofit organizations (including colleges and universities) can provide a variety of support services, advice, and even financing help. Second, business partners sometimes offer training or advice. Third, mentors and advisory boards can give business owners valuable advice and feedback on plans and decisions. Fourth, a wealth of information is available through print and online media, including business publications, blogs, and a variety of websites. Fifth, networks composed of other entrepreneurs and small business owners can provide advice, encouragement, and contacts. Fifth, business incubators and accelerators can provide the support and infrastructure that emerging businesses need to get through the early growth stage.

7. Discuss the principle sources of small-business private financing.

Bank loans are a principal source of private financing, although they are difficult for many small businesses to obtain; new mini-lenders offer opportunities for companies that need small amounts. Microlenders fill the need for smaller loans and grants in many cases. Family and friends are another source. Other alternatives include big businesses, venture capitalists, angel investors, and credit cards. Finally, the Small Business Administration, though not an actual source, can assist entrepreneurs by partially guaranteeing small bank loans.

Critical Thinking Questions - Answers

1. Describe how two of today's well known entrepreneurs have used some of the twelve characteristics of successful entrepreneurs described in the book to make their companies successful.

Whether you've chosen celebrity entrepreneurs like Jeff Bezos of Amazon or Michael Dell of Dell Inc., or up-and-coming entrepreneurs that you've read about in the business press, you should have noticed that they share some of the traits listed below. Your essay should cite the characteristics (listed below) that helped them the most and cite specific examples.

- They are highly disciplined.
- They have a high degree of confidence.
- They have plenty of physical energy and emotional stamina.
- They like to control their destiny.
- They relate well to others and have a talent for organizing team efforts in pursuit of a common goal.
- They are eager to learn whatever skills are necessary to reach their goals.
- They learn from their mistakes.
- They stay abreast of market changes.
- They are willing to exploit new opportunities.

- They are driven by a passion to succeed—but they often don't measure success in strictly financial terms.
- They think positively and are able to overcome failure and adversity; they are tenacious in pursuit of their goals.
- Contrary to popular stereotype, they are not compulsive gamblers who thrive on high-risk situations; rather, they embrace moderate risk when it is coupled with the potential for significant rewards.

2. Discuss the pros and cons of buying a franchise.

When you invest in a franchise—at least if you do your research and invest in a viable franchise—you know you are getting a viable business model, one that has worked many times before. If the franchise is well established, you get the added benefit of instant name recognition, national advertising programs, standardized quality of goods and services, and a proven formula for success. Buying a franchise also gives you access to a support network and in many cases a ready-made blueprint for building a business. For an initial investment (from a few thousand dollars to upward of a million, depending on the franchise), you get services such as site-location studies, market research, training, and technical assistance, as well as assistance with building or leasing your structure, decorating the building, purchasing supplies, and operating the business during your initial ownership phase. Some franchisors also assist franchisees in financing the initial investment.

Although franchising offers many advantages, it is not the ideal vehicle for everyone. The biggest disadvantage is the lack of control relative to other ownership options. This lack of control can affect a franchise at multiple levels. First, when you buy into a franchise system, you agree to follow the business format, and franchisors can prescribe virtually every aspect of the business, from the color of the walls to the products you can carry. In fact, if your primary purpose in owning a business is the freedom to be your own boss, franchising probably isn't the best choice because you don't have a great deal of freedom in many systems. Second, as a franchisee, you usually have little control over decisions the franchisor makes that affect the entire system. Disagreements and even lawsuits have erupted in recent years over actions taken by franchisors regarding product supplies, advertising, and pricing. Third, if the fundamental business model of the franchise system no longer works—or never worked in the first place—or if customer demand for the goods and services you sell declines, you don't have the option of changing your business in response.

Exploring the Internet - Answers

Go to www.bplans.com and click on the "Browse free sample plans" link. Select one of the plans and briefly discuss how the business in question communicates the following. Also include your thoughts on how the author of this plan could have improved the effectiveness of this plan.

- Mission and objectives
- Company and industry
- Products or services
- Market and competition
- Management
- Marketing strategy
- Design and development plans

- Operations plan
- Overall schedule
- Critical risks and problems
- Financial projections and requirements
- Exit strategy

In analyzing this business plan you will want to answer the following questions:

- Does the plan you've chosen explain the purpose of your business and what it hopes to accomplish?
- Are the origins and structure of this venture and the characteristics of its industry clear to you?
- Has the company clearly defined its product or service, and is it focusing on its unique attributes?
- Do they adequately explain how customers will benefit from using the product or service instead of those of competitors?
- Would investors see that the company understands its target market and can achieve its sales goals?
- Do they identify the strengths and weaknesses of competitors?
- Are the backgrounds and qualifications of the key management personnel included?
- Are there projections of sales and market share, and are they realistic?
- Is there a strategy for identifying and contacting customers, setting prices, providing customer services, advertising, and so forth?
- Do they offer evidence of customer acceptance, such as advance product orders?
- If products require design or development, is the nature and extent of what needs to be done, including costs and possible problems, stated?
- Is the need for facilities, equipment, and labor clearly stated?
- Does the plan identify all negative factors and discuss them honestly?
- Is there a detailed budget of startup and operating costs, as well as projections for income, expenses, and cash flow for the first three years of business?
- Does the financial data given identify the company's financing needs and potential sources?
- Do they explain how investors will be able to cash out or sell their investment, such as through a public stock offering, sale of the company, or a buyback of the investors' interest?

Chapter 7
Accounting and Financial Management

Learning Objectives
After reading this chapter, you should be able to:

1. Discuss how managers and outsiders use financial information.
2. Describe what accountants do.
3. Summarize the impact of the Sarbanes-Oxley Act.
4. State the basic accounting equation and explain the purpose of double-entry bookkeeping and the matching principle.
5. Differentiate between cash basis and accrual basis accounting.
6. Explain the purpose of the balance sheet and identify its three main sections.
7. Explain the purpose of the income statement and statement of cash flows.
8. Explain the purpose of ratio analysis and list the four main categories of financial ratios.
9. Identify the responsibilities of a financial manager.

True-False
Indicate whether the statement is generally true or false by placing a "T" or an "F" in the space provided. If it is a false statement, correct it so that it becomes a true statement.

_____ 1.   Financial accounting involves the preparation of cost analyses, profitability reports, budgets, and other information for internal use by company managers.

_____ 2.   Creditors are people or organizations that have lent a company money or have extended it credit.

_____ 3.   Private accountants are independent of the businesses, organizations, and individuals they serve.

_____ 4.   American companies whose stock is publicly traded in the United States are not required to file audited financial statements with the Securities and Exchange Commission (SEC).

_____ 5.   CPAs who work for an independent accounting firm are also known as internal auditors.

_____ 6.   FASB stands for the Federal Accounting Services Bureau.

_____ 7. The Public Company Accounting Reform and Investor Protection Act of 2002 is commonly referred to as Sarbanes-Oxley.

_____ 8. Owner's equity is the amount the business owes to its creditors, such as banks and suppliers.

_____ 9. The company's liabilities are placed before owner's equity in the accounting equation because creditors get paid first.

_____ 10. The accounting equation must always be in balance; in other words, one side of the equation must always equal the other side.

_____ 11. The cash method of accounting states that revenue is recognized when you make a sale, not when you get paid.

_____ 12. Public companies are required to keep their books on an accrual basis.

_____ 13. The income statement is a snapshot of a company's financial position on a particular date.

_____ 14. Current assets include property, plant, and equipment.

_____ 15. Accounts payable are amounts a company owes its suppliers—its "bills," in other words.

_____ 16. Accrued expenses are expenses that have been incurred but for which bills have not yet been received.

_____ 17. The process of comparing financial data from year to year in order to identify changes is known as ratio analysis.

_____ 18. A company's working capital, current assets minus current liabilities, is an important indicator of liquidity.

_____ 19. Capital structure refers to the mix of debt and equity a company uses to finance its operations.

_____ 20. The primary purpose of long-term debt financing is to ensure that a company maintains its liquidity, or its ability to meet financial obligations, as they become due.

Multiple Choice
Circle the best answer for each of the following questions.

1. Accounting is important to business because:
   a. It helps managers and owners plan and control a company's operations and make informed business decisions
   b. It helps outsiders evaluate a business
   c. Both a and c
   d. None of the above

2. Which of the following is not a recognized accounting specialty?
   a. Financial analysis
   b. Forensic accounting
   c. Cost accounting
   d. Bookkeeping

3. Which of the following issues is not a likely contributor to recent problems concerning accounting accountability?
   a. Deliberate deception of auditors by client companies
   b. The Sarbanes-Oxley Act
   c. Conflicts of interest
   d. Aggressive business practices

4. The requirement for all U.S. public companies to publish their financial statements according to GAAP allows for all of the following except:
   a. Internal auditors to omit special occurrences that they feel may distort the overall financial picture
   b. External parties to compare the financial results of one company with those of another
   c. External parties to gain a general idea of a firm's relative effectiveness
   d. External parties to evaluate a firm's standing within a particular industry

5. Which is not a requirement under Sarbanes-Oxley?
   a. Requires corporate lawyers to report evidence of financial wrongdoing
   b. Lowers the liability of corporate executives relative to the accuracy of their financial statements
   c. Prohibits external auditors from providing some non-audit services
   d. Outlaws most loans by corporations to their own directors and executives

6. Which of the following is a potential disadvantage of Sarbanes-Oxley?
    a. Cost of meeting the detailed documentation and test requirements far outweighs the benefits to investors
    b. Cost and time requirements of Sarbanes-Oxley compliance may damage American competitiveness
    c. Companies from other countries may stop listing on U.S. exchanges because the regulatory burdens are too extreme
    d. All of the above

7. Which of the following is not true about the double-entry system of bookkeeping?
    a. A debit is an increase in liabilities
    b. A credit is an increase in assets
    c. This method became popular with the wide use of computers in business in the 1970s
    d. Each transaction is entered as both a debit and a credit

8. Depreciation of a long-term asset is used to:
    a. Allocate its cost over the asset's useful life
    b. Ensure that the company's final performance would not look artificially better in the year of purchase
    c. Ensure that the company's financial performance would not look artificially worse in all future years when these assets continue to generate revenue
    d. All of the above

9. Which of the following is not one of the three primary financial statements?
    a. Balance sheet
    b. Income statement
    c. General ledger
    d. Statement of cash flows

10. The three primary financial statements do not provide information about:
    a. An organization's ability to meet current obligations
    b. The effectiveness of its sales and collection efforts
    c. An organization's effectiveness in managing its assets
    d. A forecast of future sales and profits

11. By reading a company's balance sheet you should be able to determine:
    a. It's profitability for a given period
    b. The extent of its assets
    c. How cash was used during a given period
    d. All of the above

12. Which of the following would not be considered an "asset" for accounting purposes?
    a. Cash
    b. A good management team
    c. Equipment
    d. Intellectual property

13. Which of the following contributes to "owner's equity"?
    a. The total value of all the shares
    b. Retained earnings
    c. The total value of all loans, leases, and bonds held by the company
    d. Both a and b

14. A company's income statement will summarize all of the following except:
    a. Expenses
    b. Net income
    c. Liabilities
    d. Revenues

15. By analyzing a company's financial statements you should be able to:
    a. Evaluate the financial health of the organization.
    b. Make business decisions.
    c. Spot opportunities for improvements.
    d. All of the above

16. Which of the following is not a standard type of financial ratio?
    a. Sales
    b. Profitability
    c. Liquidity
    d. Leverage

17. Which of the following is a type of liquidity ratio?
    a. Earnings per share
    b. Inventory turnover ratio
    c. Current ratio
    d. Debt-to-equity ratio

18. Which of the following is not a working capital account?
    a. Cash
    b. Net income
    c. Accounts payable
    d. Inventory

Match the Terms and Concepts with Their Definitions

A.   accounting
B.   accounting equation
C.   accounts payable
D.   accounts receivable
E.   accounts receivable turnover ratio
F.   accrual basis
G.   activity ratios
H.   assets
I.   audit
J.   balance sheet
K.   bookkeeping
L.   budget
M.   calendar year
N.   capital budgeting
O.   capital investments
P.   cash basis
Q.   certified management accountants (CMAs)
R.   certified public accountants (CPAs)
S.   close the books
T.   controller
U.   cost of goods sold
V.   credit
W.   current assets
X.   current liabilities
Y.   current ratio
Z.   debit
AA.   debit ratios
BB.   debt-to-equity ratio
CC.   debt-to-total-assets ratio
DD.   depreciation
EE.   double-entry bookkeeping
FF.   earnings per share

GG.   expenses
HH.   financial accounting
II.   financial control
JJ.   financial management
KK.   financial plan
LL.   fiscal year
MM.   fixed assets
NN.   general expenses
OO.   generally accepted accounting principles (GAAP)
PP.   gross profit
QQ.   income statement
RR.   inventory turnover ratio
SS.   liabilities
TT.   liquidity ratios
UU.   long-term liabilities
VV.   management accounting
WW.   marketable securities
XX.   matching principle
YY.   net income
ZZ.   operating expenses
AAA.   owner's equity
BBB.   private accountants
CCC.   profitability ratios
DDD.   quick ratio
EEE.   ratio analysis
FFF.   retained earnings
GGG.   return on investment (ROI)
HHH.   return on sales
III.   revenues
JJJ.   Sarbanes-Oxley
KKK.   selling expenses
LLL.   statement of cash flows
MMM. working capital

_____   1.   Measuring, interpreting, and communicating financial information to support internal and external decision making

_____   2.   Preparing data for use by managers within the organization

_____   3.   Preparing financial information for users outside the organization

_____ 4. Recordkeeping, clerical aspect of accounting

_____ 5. Highest-ranking accountant in a company, responsible for overseeing all accounting functions

_____ 6. Professionally licensed accountants who meet certain requirements for education and experience and who pass a comprehensive examination

_____ 7. Accountants who have fulfilled the requirements for certification as specialists in management accounting

_____ 8. Formal evaluation of the fairness and reliability of a client's financial statements

_____ 9. Professionally approved U.S. standards and practices used by accountants in the preparation of financial statements

_____ 10. Comprehensive legislation, passed in the wake of Enron and other scandals, designed to improve integrity and accountability of financial information

_____ 11. Anything of value owned or leased by a business

_____ 12. Claims against a firm's assets by creditors

_____ 13. Portion of a company's assets that belongs to the owners after obligations to all creditors have been met; called shareholders' or stockholders' in publicly traded companies

_____ 14. Assets equal liabilities plus owners' equity

_____ 15. Way of recording financial transactions that requires two entries for every transaction so that the accounting equation is always kept in balance

_____ 16. An increase in liabilities

_____ 17. In bookkeeping, an increase in assets

_____ 18. Fundamental principle requiring that expenses incurred in producing revenue be deducted from the revenues they generate during an accounting period

_____ 19. Accounting method in which revenue is recorded when a sale is made and expense is recorded when it is incurred

_____ 20. Accounting method in which revenue is recorded when payment is received and expense is recorded when cash is paid

_____ 21.   Accounting procedure for systematically spreading the cost of a tangible asset over its estimated useful life

_____ 22.   The act of transferring net revenue and expense account balances to retained earnings for the period

_____ 23.   Statement of a firm's financial position on a particular date; also known as a statement of financial position

_____ 24.   Twelve-month accounting period that begins on January 1 and ends on December 31

_____ 25.   Any 12 consecutive months used as an accounting period

_____ 26.   Cash and items that can be turned into cash within one year

_____ 27.   Assets retained for long-term use, such as land, buildings, machinery, and equipment; also referred to as property, plant, and equipment

_____ 28.   Stocks, bonds, and other investments that can be turned into cash quickly

_____ 29.   Amounts that are currently due to a company

_____ 30.   Obligations that must be met within a year

_____ 31.   Obligations that fall due more than a year from the date of the balance sheet

_____ 32.   Short-term credit or debt amounts that a company owes its suppliers; the company's "bills," in other words

_____ 33.   The portion of shareholders' equity earned by the company but not distributed to its owners in the form of dividends

_____ 34.   Financial record of a company's revenues, expenses, and profits over a given period of time

_____ 35.   Amount earned from sales of goods or services and inflow from miscellaneous sources such as interest, rent, and royalties

_____ 36.   Costs created in the process of generating revenues

_____ 37.   Profit earned or loss incurred by a firm, determined by subtracting expenses from revenues; also called the bottom line

_____ 38. Cost of producing or acquiring a company's products for sale during a given period

_____ 39. Amount remaining when the cost of goods sold is deducted from net sales; also known as gross margin

_____ 40. All costs of operation that are not included under cost of goods sold

_____ 41. All the operating expenses associated with marketing goods or services

_____ 42. Operating expenses, such as office and administrative expenses, not directly associated with creating or marketing a good or a service

_____ 43. Statement of a firm's cash receipts and cash payments that presents information on its sources and uses of cash

_____ 44. Use of quantitative measures to evaluate a firm's financial performance

_____ 45. Ratios that measure the overall financial performance of a firm

_____ 46. Ratio between net income after taxes and net sales; also known as profit margin

_____ 47. Ratio between net income after taxes and total owners' equity; also known as return on equity

_____ 48. Measure of profitability calculated by dividing net income after taxes by the average number of shares of common stock outstanding

_____ 49. Ratios that measure a firm's ability to meet its short-term obligations when they are due

_____ 50. Current assets minus current liabilities

_____ 51. Measure of a firm's short-term liquidity, calculated by dividing current assets by current liabilities

_____ 52. Measure of a firm's short-term liquidity, calculated by adding cash, marketable securities, and receivables, then dividing that sum by current liabilities; also known as the acid-test ratio

_____ 53. Ratios that measure the effectiveness of the firm's use of its resources

_____ 54. Measure of the time a company takes to turn its inventory into sales, calculated by dividing cost of goods sold by the average value of inventory for a period

_____ 55.   Measure of time a company takes to turn its accounts receivable into cash, calculated by dividing sales by the average value of accounts receivable for a period

_____ 56.   Ratios that measure a firm's reliance on debt financing of its operations (sometimes called leverage ratios)

_____ 57.   Measure of the extent to which a business is financed by debt as opposed to invested capital, calculated by dividing the company's total liabilities by owners' equity

_____ 58.   Measure of a firm's ability to carry long-term debt, calculated by dividing total liabilities by total assets

_____ 59.   Effective acquisition and use of money

_____ 60.   A forecast of financial requirements and the financing sources to be used

_____ 61.   Planning and control tool that reflects expected revenues, operating expenses, and cash receipts and outlays

_____ 62.   The process of analyzing and adjusting the basic financial plan to correct for forecasted events that do not materialize

_____ 63.   Money paid to acquire something of permanent value in a business

_____ 64.   Process for evaluating proposed investments in select projects that provide the best long-term financial return

_____ 65.   Professionals who work for businesses, government agencies, or nonprofit organizations

Learning Objectives—Short Answer or Essay Questions

1.   Discuss how managers and outsiders use financial information.

2.   Describe what accountants do.

3.   Summarize the impact of the Sarbanes-Oxley Act.

4.   State the basic accounting equation and explain the purpose of double-entry bookkeeping and the matching principle.

5.   Differentiate between cash basis and accrual basis accounting.

6.   Explain the purpose of the balance sheet and identify its three main sections.

7.   Explain the purpose of the income statement and statement of cash flows.

8.   Explain the purpose of ratio analysis and list the four main categories of financial ratios.

9.   Identify the responsibilities of a financial manager.

Critical Thinking Questions

1.   Discuss some reasons public accounting has come under intense public and regulatory scrutiny, and name some measures that companies and accounting firms can take to solve these issues.

2. Compare and contrast the use of debt and equity financing.

Exploring the Internet

Search the Internet to find the most recent annual report for a Fortune 500 company. (You can find a list of these companies at www.fortune500.com.) Read the report, and describe what the numbers in the report are telling you. Do the letters or other written sections support or contradict what you see in the numbers? Explain.

True-False – Answers

1. False	8. False	15. True
2. True	9. True	16. True
3. False	10. True	17. False
4. False	11. False	18. True
5. False	12. True	19. True
6. False	13. False	20. False
7. True	14. False	

Multiple Choice – Answers

1. C	7. C	13. D
2. D	8. A	14. C
3. B	9. C	15. A
4. A	10. D	16. C
5. B	11. B	17. B
6. D	12. B	

Match the Terms and Concepts with their Definitions – Answers

1. A	23. J	45. CCC
2. VV	24. M	46. HHH
3. HH	25. LL	47. GGG
4. K	26. W	48. FF
5. T	27. MM	49. TT
6. R	28. WW	50. MMM
7. Q	29. D	51. Y
8. I	30. X	52. DDD
9. OO	31. UU	53. G
10. JJJ	32. C	54. RR
11. H	33. FFF	55. E
12. SS	34. QQ	56. AA
13. AAA	35. III	57. BB
14. B	36. GG	58. CC
15. EE	37. YY	59. JJ
16. Z	38. U	60. KK
17. V	39. PP	61. L
18. XX	40. ZZ	62. II
19. F	41 KKK	63. O
20. P	42. NN	64. N
21. DD	43. LLL	65. BBB
22. S	44. EEE	

Learning Objectives – Short Answer or Essay Question – Answers

1. **Discuss how managers and outsiders use financial information.**

   Managers use financial information to control a company's operation and to make informed business decisions. Outsiders use financial information to evaluate whether a business is creditworthy or a good investment. Specifically, banks want to know if a business is able to pay back a loan, investors want to know if the company is earning a profit, and governments want to be assured the company is paying the proper amount of taxes.

2. **Describe what accountants do.**

   Accountants design and install accounting systems, prepare financial statements, analyze and interpret financial information, prepare financial forecasts and budgets, prepare tax returns, interpret tax law, compute and analyze production costs, evaluate a company's performance, and analyze the financial implications of business decisions. In addition to these functions, accountants help managers improve business procedures, plan for the future, evaluate product performance, analyze the firm's profitability, and design and install computer systems. Auditors are licensed certified public accountants who review accounting records and processes to assess whether they conform to GAAP and whether the company's financial statements fairly present the company's financial position and operating results.

3. Summarize the impact of the Sarbanes-Oxley Act.

Sarbanes-Oxley introduced a number of rules covering the way publicly traded companies manage and report their finances, including restricting loans to directors and executives, creating a new board to oversee public auditors, requiring corporate lawyers to report financial wrongdoing, requiring CEOs and CFOs to sign financial statements under oath, and requiring companies to document their financial systems.

4. State the basic accounting equation, and explain the purpose of double-entry bookkeeping and the matching principle.

The basic accounting equation is Assets = Liabilities + Owners' Equity. Double-entry bookkeeping is a system of recording financial transactions to keep the accounting equation in balance. The matching principle makes sure that expenses incurred in producing revenues are deducted from the revenue they generated during the same accounting period.

5. Differentiate between cash basis and accrual basis accounting.

Cash basis accounting recognizes revenue at the time payment is received, whereas accrual basis accounting recognizes revenue at the time of sale, even if payment is not made.

6. Explain the purpose of the balance sheet, and identify its three main sections.

The balance sheet provides a snapshot of the business at a particular point in time. It shows the size of the company, the major assets owned, how the assets are financed, and the amount of owners' investment in the business. Its three main sections are assets, liabilities, and owners' equity.

7. Explain the purpose of the income statement and the statement of cash flows.

The income statement reflects the results of operations over a period of time. It gives a general sense of a company's size and performance. The statement of cash flows shows how a company's cash was received and spent in three areas: operations, investments, and financing. It gives a general sense of the amount of cash created or consumed by daily operations, fixed assets, investments, and debt over a period of time.

8. **Explain the purpose of ratio analysis, and list the four main categories of financial ratios.**

Financial ratios provide information for analyzing the health and future prospects of a business. Ratios facilitate financial comparisons among different-size companies and between a company and industry averages. Most of the important ratios fall into one of four categories: profitability ratios, which show how well the company generates profits; liquidity ratios, which measure the company's ability to pay its short-term obligations; activity ratios, which analyze how well a company is managing its assets; and debt ratios, which measure a company's ability to pay its long-term debt.

9. **Identify the responsibilities of a financial manager.**

The responsibilities of a financial manager include developing and implementing a firm's financial plan, monitoring a firm's cash flow and deciding how to create or use excess funds, budgeting for current and future expenditures, recommending specific investments, raising capital to finance the enterprise for future growth, and interacting with banks and capital markets.

Critical Thinking Questions - Answers

1. **Discuss some reasons public accounting has come under intense public and regulatory scrutiny, and name some measures that companies and accounting firms can take to solve these issues.**

There are many issues that have contributed to this dilemma, but you should have considered the following factors in your analysis:

- Deliberate deception by corporate clients. Auditors maintain that in many cases it is impossible to detect deliberately misleading bookkeeping, and it is unfair to hold them accountable when they do not.

- Changes in accounting practices. In the past, auditors used a labor-intensive process of sifting through thousands of transactions to determine if bookkeeping entries were correct. Now they focus on analyzing the computerized bookkeeping programs and internal controls. While this approach prevents low-level employees from swiping petty cash, it can't always catch executives who shift millions or billions around using creative accounting schemes.

- Conflict of interest. Cozy relationships between auditors and clients along with lucrative consulting contracts create a conflict of interest and discourage some auditors from examining corporate books closely enough or challenging CEOs when potential irregularities surface.

- Overly aggressive business practices. In 1991, the AICPA changed its code of conduct to allow tax accountants to charge performance-based fees, meaning that firms could charge a percentage of the money they saved clients by lowering their taxes. The IRS and industry insiders say this spawned a rash of overly aggressive tax shelters throughout the 1990s. After the IRS finally got its arms around the problem, it started banning these shelters, fining accountants who sold them, and recovering back taxes from clients who used them. Some of these clients are suing their accountants, claiming they were misled.

There is also tremendous pressure on CEOs to show positive performance for their firm, and it is believed by some that some CEOs may be willing to behave unethically in order to meet their goals.

2. Compare and contrast the use of debt and equity financing.

Few businesses are able to reach their goals without receiving outside financial assistance somewhere along the way. As you can imagine, financing an enterprise is a complex undertaking. The process begins by assessing the firm's financing needs and determining whether funds are needed for the short or the long term. Managers must also assess the cost of obtaining financing and weigh the advantages and disadvantages of financing through debt or equity, taking into consideration the firm's special needs and circumstances. Choosing a company's capital structure—the mix of debt and equity—is one of the most important decisions top managers ever make.

Debt financing refers to acquiring funds through borrowing; that is, taking on debt. A creditor agrees to lend money to a debtor in exchange for repayment, with accumulated interest, at some future date. Loans can be secured or unsecured. *Secured loans* are those backed by something of value, known as *collateral,* which may be seized by the lender if the borrower fails to repay the loan. The most common types of collateral are accounts receivable, inventories, and property such as marketable securities, buildings, and other assets. *Unsecured loans* are loans that require no collateral. Instead, the lender relies on the general credit record and the earning power of the borrower.

Equity financing is achieved by selling shares of a company's stock. "Going public" is an effective method of raising needed capital, but it can be an expensive and time-consuming process with no guarantee you will get the amount of money you need.

When choosing between debt and equity financing, you should weigh the advantages and disadvantages of each. In addition to considering whether the financing is for the short or the long term and assessing the cost of the financing, such as interest, fees, and other charges, you must also evaluate your desire for ownership control. Two of the biggest benefits of debt financing are (1) the lender does not gain an ownership interest in the business, and (2) a firm's obligations are limited to repaying the loan. In contrast, equity financing involves an exchange of money for a share of business ownership. It allows firms to obtain funds without pledging to repay a specific amount of money at a particular time, but in exchange for this benefit the firm must give up some ownership control.

Exploring the Internet

Search the Internet to find the most recent annual report for a Fortune 500 company. (You can find a list of these companies at www.fortune500.com.) Read the report, and describe what the numbers in the report are telling you. Do the letters or other written sections support or contradict what you see in the numbers? Explain.

Check out the trend in the company's working capital (the difference between current assets and current liabilities). If working capital is shrinking, it could mean trouble. One possibility: The company may not be able to keep dividends growing rapidly. Another important number to analyze is earnings per share. Management can boost earnings by selling off a plant or by cutting the budget for research or advertising. See the footnotes; they often tell the whole story. If earnings are down only because of a change in accounting, maybe that's good! The company owes less tax and has more money in its pocket. If earnings are up, maybe that's bad. They may be up because of a special windfall that will not happen again next year. One good indicator is the trend in net sales. If sales increases are starting to slow, the company may be in trouble.

High and rising debt, relative to equity, may be no problem for a growing business. But it shows weakness in a company that is leveling out. So get out your calculator and divide long-term liabilities by shareholders' equity. That is the debt-to-equity ratio. A high ratio means the company borrows a lot of money to fund its growth. That's okay—if sales grow too, and if there's enough cash on hand to meet the payments. But if sales fall, watch out. The whole enterprise may slowly sink.

You should find two letters, one from the third-party auditor and one from the CEO or chairman of the board. The third-party auditor will tell you right off the bat if the report conforms with generally accepted accounting principles, and will briefly discuss the auditing process and any assumptions that were made or limitations encountered.

The letter from the CEO/chairman should tell you how the company fared this year, but more important, the letter should tell you why. Keep an eye out for sentences that start with "Except for . . ." and "Despite the . . ." They are clues to potential problems. The chair's letter should also give you insights into the company's future. For example, look for what is new in each line of business. Is management positioning the company for new market developments and changing competition?

Remember, one ratio, one annual report, one letter will not tell you much. You have to compare. Is the company's debt-to-equity ratio better or worse than it used to be? Better or worse than the industry norms?

Chapter 8
Banking and Securities

Learning Objectives
After reading this chapter, you should be able to:

1. Highlight the functions, characteristics, and common forms of money.
2. Discuss the responsibilities and insurance methods of the FDIC.
3. Discuss how industry deregulation and the repeal of the Glass-Steagall Act are affecting the banking industry.
4. Highlight the distinguishing features of common stock, preferred stock, bonds, and mutual funds.
5. Explain the advantages of index funds.
6. Discuss the importance of establishing investment objectives and identify five factors to consider when making investment choices.
7. Explain how government regulation of securities trading tries to protect investors.

True-False
Indicate whether the statement is generally true or false by placing a "T" or an "F" in the space provided. If it is a false statement, correct it so that it becomes a true statement.

_____ 1. Currency is anything generally accepted as a means of paying for goods and services.

_____ 2. Money market accounts and certificates of deposit are types of savings accounts that may require advance notice or impose withdrawal limits.

_____ 3. Thrifts are nonprofit member-owned organizations that take deposits only from members, such as one company's employees or one union's members or another designated group.

_____ 4. Investment banks allow investors to buy and sell stocks, bonds, and other investments. Many also offer checking accounts, high-paying savings accounts, and loans to buy securities.

_____ 5. The Depository Institutions Deregulation and Monetary Control Act of 1980 is a law that deregulated banking and made it possible for all financial institutions to offer a wider range of services.

_____ 6. Banks are required to file suspicious activity reports (SARs) with government authorities whenever they detect types of financial transactions flagged by the USA PATRIOT Act and similar legislation.

_____ 7. The 1999 Financial Services Modernization Act repealed the Glass-Steagall Act of 1933 and portions of the 1956 Bank Holding Act, thereby letting banks into the securities and insurance businesses.

_____ 8. Owners of a common stock can vote to elect the company's board of directors, vote on other important corporate issues, and receive dividend payments from the company's profits.

_____ 9. Owners of common stock enjoy higher dividends and a better claim (after creditors) on assets if the corporation fails than owners of preferred stock.

_____ 10. Bonds are a type of financing.

_____ 11. Debentures are a type of secured bond backed by collateral owned by the issuing corporation.

_____ 12. Mutual funds are particularly well suited for investors who wish to diversify their investment over a variety of securities.

_____ 13. Indexed funds have a manager or team of managers that chooses which securities to buy based on an established investment strategy.

_____ 14. Stocks that sell on the NYSE or any other exchange are said to be listed on that exchange.

_____ 15. The NASDAQ is a type of auction exchange.

_____ 16. The SEC's mission to ensure full and fair disclosure means that all investors should have access to all the relevant information they need.

_____ 17. A margin call notice from the broker means you need to put more cash in your account or sell your stock if you don't have the cash – even if that means selling at a steep loss.

_____ 18. If stock prices have been rising over a long period, the industry and the media will often describe this situation as a bear market.

Multiple Choice

Circle the best answer for each of the following questions.

1. To be an effective medium of exchange, money must have all these important characteristics except:
    a. It must be divisible (ease to divide into smaller denominations)
    b. Portable (easy to carry)
    c. Difficult to counterfeit
    d. All of the above

2. Money must perform all of these functions except:
    a. It must serve as a medium of exchange
    b. It must consist of bills (paper money) and coins to facilitate consumer exchange
    c. It must serve as a measure of value so that you do not have to negotiate the relative worth of dissimilar items every time you buy something
    d. It must serve as a temporary store of value

3. Which of the following is an advantage of using a credit card versus other purchasing options?
    a. It allows card users a better way to track and analyze their spending
    b. It deducts cash directly from the user's checking account
    c. Both a and b
    d. None of the above

4. Which of the following would be considered a non-deposit institution?
    a. A commercial bank
    b. A pension fund
    c. A credit union
    d. A savings and loan association

5. Which is true about the FDIC?
    a. It insures individuals for up to $500,000
    b. It is funded by collecting premiums from account holders
    c. It insures banks for up to $100,000 per account
    d. All of the above

6. Which of the following does not match the type of bank charter with the agency that oversees it?
    a. Privately chartered banks; the Federal Office of Banking and Finance
    b. State-chartered banks; individual state agencies
    c. Nationally chartered banks; the Federal Office of the Comptroller of Currency
    d. Thrifts; the Federal Office of Thrift Supervision

7. Which of the following is not a reason there are fewer banks (main offices) in the U.S. today than there were in the depths of the Great Depression?
   a. Competitive pressure
   b. Mergers and combinations
   c. Lower per capita income
   d. Financial difficulties

8. Which are the three principle types of securities?
   a. Stocks, bonds, and cash
   b. Stocks, bonds, and mutual funds
   c. Stocks, bonds, and loans
   d. Treasury bills, Treasury notes, and Treasury bonds

9. Which of the following is true about the stock shares of a corporation?
   a. The board of directors determines the maximum number of shares into which the business can be divided
   b. All shares created are called authorized shares
   c. The shares sold are called issued shares
   d. All of the above

10. All of the following are true about high-yield bonds except:
    a. They have received a low rating from one of the rating agencies
    b. They have received a high rating from one of the rating agencies
    c. They offer a higher interest rate
    d. They are also known as junk bonds

11. Why do convertible bonds typically pay a lower interest rate than other bonds?
    a. Because they can be converted into shares of common stock
    b. Because they can be converted into cash
    c. Because they have a higher risk than other types of bonds
    d. None of the above

12. Which of the following Treasury securities take the longest time to mature?
    a. Treasury bills
    b. Treasury notes
    c. Treasury bonds
    d. Savings bonds

13. Which of the following organizations could not issue a municipal bond?
    a. A school district
    b. A state government
    c. A municipality
    d. A private corporation

14. A closed-end mutual fund:
    a. Raises all its money at once by distributing a fixed number of shares that trade on stock exchanges
    b. Is an open-ended mutual fund that closes to new investors at some point, either temporarily or permanently
    c. Issues additional shares as new investors ask to buy them
    d. Charges no fees to buy or sell shares

15. A mutual fund that is considered to be an income fund will typically:
    a. Invest in stocks of rapidly growing companies
    b. Invest in securities that pay high dividends and interest
    c. Invest in a carefully chosen mix of stocks and bonds
    d. Invest in companies within a particular industry

16. Which of the following is not considered a type of securities fraud?
    a. Insider trading
    b. Inaccurate or incomplete disclosure of information
    c. Market manipulation (buying or selling in ways designed to influence prices)
    d. None of the above

17. Managing an investment portfolio to gain the highest rates of return while reducing risk as much as possible is known as:
    a. Diversification
    b. Value investing
    c. Asset allocation
    d. Margin trading

18. A market order:
    a. Tells the broker to buy or sell at the best price that can be negotiated at the moment
    b. Specifies the highest price you are willing to pay when buying or the lowest price at which you are willing to sell
    c. Tells the broker to sell if the price of your security drops to or below the price you set, protecting you from losing more money if prices are dropping. You can also place a time limit on your orders
    d. Instructs the broker to leave the order open until you cancel it

Match the Terms and Concepts with Their Definitions

A.	auction exchange		H.	checks
B.	automated teller machines		I.	convertible bonds
C.	bear market		J.	credit cards
D.	bond		K.	currency
E.	broker		L.	day order
F.	bull market		M.	dealer exchange
G.	capital gains		N.	debentures

O.   debit cards
P.   demand deposit
Q.   discretionary order
R.   electronic funds transfer systems
S.   general obligation bond
T.   Treasury bills
U.   institutional investor
V.   line of credit
W.   margin trading
X.   market indexes
Y.   speculators
Z.   asset allocation
AA.   money
BB.   Treasury notes
CC.   municipal bonds
DD.   mutual funds
EE.   NASDAQ
FF.   open order

GG.   over-the-counter (OTC) market
HH.   investment portfolio
II.   price-earnings ratio
JJ.   primary market
KK.   principal
LL.   revenue bond
MM. secondary market
NN.   secured bonds
OO.   securities
PP.   short selling
QQ.   stock exchanges
RR.   diversification
SS.   stock split
TT.   stop order
UU.   time deposits
VV.   Treasury bonds
WW. Smart cards
XX.   U.S. savings bonds

1.   _____ Anything generally accepted as a means of paying for goods and services

2.   _____ Bills and coins that make up a country's cash money

3.   _____ Money that can be used by the customer at any time, such as checking accounts

4.   _____ Bank accounts that pay interest and require advance notice before money can be withdrawn

5.   _____ Written orders that tell the user's bank to pay a specific amount to a particular individual or business

6.   _____ Plastic cards that allow the user to buy now and repay the loaned amount at a future date

7.   _____ Plastic cards that allow the bank to take money from the user's demand-deposit account and transfer it to a retailer's account

8.   _____ Cards with embedded computer chips that store bank account amounts and personal data

9.   _____ Arrangement in which the financial institution makes money available for use at any time after the loan has been approved

10.   _____ Electronic terminals that permit people to perform basic banking transactions 24 hours a day without a human teller

11. _____Computerized systems for completing financial transactions

12. _____Investments such as stocks, bonds, options, futures, and commodities

13. _____Increase in the number of shares of ownership that each stock certificate represents, at a proportionate drop in each share's value

14. _____Method of funding in which the issuer borrows from an investor and provides a written promise to make regular interest payments and repay the borrowed amount in the future

15. _____Amount of money a corporation borrows from an investor through the sale of a bond

16. _____Bonds backed by specific assets that will be given to bondholders if the borrowed amount is not repaid

17. _____Corporate bonds backed only by the reputation of the issuer

18. _____Corporate bonds that can be exchanged at the owner's discretion into common stock of the issuing company

19. _____Short-term debt securities issued by the federal government

20. _____Debt securities issued by the federal government that are repaid within 1 to 10 years after issuance

21. _____Debt securities issued by the federal government that are repaid more than 10 years after issuance

22. _____Debt instruments sold by the federal government in a variety of amounts

23. _____Bonds issued by city, state, and government agencies to fund public services

24. _____Municipal bond that is backed by the government's authority to collect taxes

25. _____Municipal bond backed by revenue generated from the projects it is financing

26. _____Return that investors receive when they sell a security for a higher price than the purchase price

27. _____Financial organization pooling money to invest in diversified blends of stocks, bonds, or other securities

28. _____Market where firms sell new securities issued publicly for the first time

29. _____Market where subsequent owners trade previously issued shares of stocks and bonds

30. _____Location where traders buy and sell stocks and bonds

31. _____Centralized marketplace where securities are traded by specialists on behalf of investors

32. _____Network of dealers who trade securities on computerized linkups rather than a trading floor

33. _____National over-the-counter securities trading network

34. _____Decentralized marketplace where securities are bought and sold by dealers out of their own inventories

35. _____Investors who make risky investment decisions in anticipation of making large profits quickly

36. _____Assortment of investment instruments

37. _____Method of shifting investments within a portfolio to adapt them to the current investment environment and investor objectives

38. _____Assembling investment portfolios in such a way that a loss in one investment won't cripple the value of the entire portfolio .

39. _____An expert who has passed specific tests and is registered to trade securities for investors

40. _____An order to sell a stock when its price falls to a particular point to limit an investor's losses

41. _____Limit order that does not expire at the end of a trading day

42. _____Any order to buy or sell a security that automatically expires if not executed on the day the order is placed

43. _____Market order that allows the broker to decide when to trade a security

44. _____Borrowing money from brokers to buy stock, paying interest on the borrowed money, and leaving the stock with the broker as collateral

45. _____Selling stock borrowed from a broker with the intention of buying it back later at a lower price, repaying the broker, and keeping the profit

46. _____Rising stock market

47. _____Falling stock market

48. _____Companies and other organizations that invest significant amounts of money, often funds entrusted to them by others

49. _____Measures of market activity calculated from the prices of a selection of securities

50. _____ Ratio calculated by dividing a stock's market price by its earnings per share over a 12-month period (usually the previous 12 months)

Learning Objectives—Short Answer or Essay Questions

1. Highlight the functions, characteristics, and common forms of money.

2. Discuss the responsibilities and insurance methods of the FDIC.

3. Discuss how industry deregulation and the repeal of the Glass-Steagall Act are affecting the banking industry.

4. Highlight the distinguishing features of common stock, preferred stock, bonds, and mutual funds.

5. Explain the advantages of index funds.

6. Discuss the importance of establishing investment objectives and identify five factors to consider when making investment choices.

7. Explain how government regulation of securities trading tries to protect investors.

Critical Thinking Questions

1. Discuss current trends in electronic banking and how they affect both consumers and the banking industry.

2. Explain how institutional investors interact and influence the securities market.

Exploring the Internet

Visit the SEC website at **www.sec.gov**, then click on "Filings & Forms (EDGAR)."
Describe what you find there and discuss why this is a valuable service to companies and investors.

True-False—Answers

1. False	8. True	15. False
2. True	9. False	16. True
3. False	10. False	17. True
4. False	11. False	18. False
5. True	12. True	
6. True	13. False	
7. True	14. True	

Multiple Choice—Answers

1. D	8. B	15. B
2. B	9. D	16. D
3. A	10. B	17. C
4. B	11. A	18. A
5. C	12. C	
6. A	13. D	
7. C	14. A	

Match the Terms and Concepts with Their Definitions - Answers

1.	AA	18.	I	35.	Y
2.	K	19.	T	36.	HH
3.	P	20.	BB	37.	Z
4.	UU	21.	VV	38.	RR
5.	H	22.	XX	39.	E
6.	J	23.	CC	40.	TT
7.	O	24.	S	41.	FF
8.	WW	25.	LL	42.	L
9.	V	26.	G	43.	Q
10.	B	27.	DD	44.	W
11.	R	28.	JJ	45.	PP
12.	OO	29.	MM	46.	F
13.	SS	30.	QQ	47.	C
14.	D	31.	A	48.	U
15.	KK	32.	GG	49.	X
16.	NN	33.	EE	50.	II
17.	N	34.	M		

Learning Objectives—Short Answer or Essay Question - Answers

1. **Highlight the functions, characteristics, and common forms of money.**
Money functions as a medium of exchange, a measure of value, and a store of value. It must be divisible, portable, durable, stable, and difficult to counterfeit. Common forms of money include currency, such as coins, bills, traveler's checks, cashier's checks, and money orders; demand deposits, such as checking accounts; and time deposits, such as savings accounts, certificates of deposit, and money-market deposit accounts.

2. **Discuss the responsibilities and insurance methods of the FDIC.**

   The Federal Deposit Insurance Corporation is a federal insurance program that protects deposits in member banks. Banks pay premiums to the FDIC, which insures funds on deposit with a particular bank for up to $100,000 in case of bank failure. The FDIC supervises the Bank Insurance Fund, which covers deposits in commercial banks and savings banks, and the Savings Association Insurance Fund, which covers deposits in savings and loan associations.

3. **Discuss how deregulation and the repeal of the Glass-Steagall Act are affecting the banking industry.**

   Deregulation and the repeal of the Glass-Steagall Act are fueling a raft of mega-mergers among banks, insurance companies, and brokerage firms and increasing the competition among these institutions. As a result, the line between the types of financial services offered by banks, securities brokers, and insurance companies is blurring. Meanwhile, community banks are stepping in to fill a void created by bank consolidations by focusing on the needs of local customers (generally, small businesses).

4. **Highlight the distinguishing features of common stock, preferred stock, bonds, and mutual funds.**

   Common stock gives shareholders an ownership interest in the company, the right to elect directors and vote on important issues, and the chance to earn dividends and share in the fortunes of the company—while limiting the shareholder's liability to the price paid for the shares. Preferred stock gives shareholders a higher dividend than common stock and a preferred claim over creditors if the corporation fails. Special types of preferred stock have certain privileges. Bonds are long-term loans investors make to the issuing entity in return for a stated interest amount. The loan or principal is paid back to the bondholder over the life of the bond. Bonds may be secured, unsecured, or convertible. They may be issued by corporations or federal, state, city, and local agencies. Mutual funds are pools

110

of money drawn from many investors to buy a variety of stocks, bonds, and other marketable securities. The primary benefit of this investment is diversification.

5. Explain the advantages of index funds.

Index mutual funds offer three potential advantages: lower cost (less of the investors' money is consumed by fees), simple diversification (with even a small investment, investors' money is spread across many stocks and often multiple industries and geographic regions), and better performance than the majority of actively managed funds.

6. Discuss the importance of establishing investment objectives, and identify five factors to consider when making investment choices.

Adding up all the stocks, bonds, mutual funds, real estate possibilities, and other vehicles, investors face literally millions of competing investment opportunities spread across a wide range of potential risk and reward levels. Some investment options are appropriate for some investing objectives, but completely inappropriate for others. Therefore, establishing objectives first is essential to making smart investment choices. The five factors investors should always consider are income, growth, safety, liquidity, and tax consequences.

7. Explain how government regulation of securities trading tries to protect investors.

The government tries to prevent fraud in the securities markets by requiring companies to file registration papers, fulfill certain requirements, and file periodic information reports so that investors receive accurate information. Government regulations also control the listing of companies on stock exchanges and prohibit such fraudulent acts as improper release of information, insider trading, stock scams, and other acts designed to deceive investors.

Critical Thinking Questions - Answers

1. Discuss current trends in electronic banking and how they affect both consumers and the banking industry.

Most deposit institutions offer electronic banking services that may be conducted from sites other than the bank's physical location. The most visible form of electronic banking consists of the automated teller machines (ATMs) now located everywhere from street corners to shopping malls to airports. By linking with regional, national, and international ATM networks, banks let customers withdraw cash far from home, make deposits, and handle other transactions. Some bank ATMs also provide web access, allowing customers to perform a wide variety of online banking tasks, from paying bills to transferring funds between accounts.

Electronic funds transfer systems (EFTS) are computerized systems that allow users to conduct financial transactions efficiently from remote locations. Many employees take advantage of EFTS when their employers use direct deposit to transfer wages directly into employees' bank accounts. This procedure saves employers and employees the worry and headache of handling large amounts of cash. Banks sometimes provide discounted service fees for customers who use direct deposit, since handling payroll transactions electronically is less expensive.

In addition to ATMs and EFTS, most major banks and many smaller financial institutions now offer a variety of online banking services. Services typically offered including the ability to transfer money between accounts, check account balances, pay bills, and apply for loans. Some banks also offer personal financial management services, such as the ability to establish household budgets and track spending by categories. Approaching the same challenge from the opposite direction, Intuit (maker of the popular Quicken and QuickBooks financial software) is beginning to integrate its product with online banking services as well.

One of the newest areas of innovation in electronic banking is mobile banking, whereby customers can access their accounts with their mobile phones. For example, through special software downloaded to their phones, Citibank customers can view account information, pay bills, and transfer funds. Future possibilities include retail checkout systems that can detect the presence of suitably equipped mobile phones and deduct purchase amounts from the user's bank account.

2. Explain how institutional investors interact and influence the securities market.

Institutional investors—such as pension funds, insurance companies, investment companies, banks, and colleges and universities—buy and sell securities in large quantities. Because these institutions have such large pools of money to work with, their investment decisions have a major impact on the marketability of a company's shares as well as the overall behavior of the securities market. If the stock market is down on heavy volume (that is, if prices are moving downward and a lot of trading is going on), institutional investors may be trying to sell before prices go down further—a bearish sign. At the same time, don't think that you should necessarily mimic institutional investors; they usually don't pay attention to smaller stocks that could fit nicely in a growth-oriented portfolio, for instance.

Exploring the Internet - Answers

**Visit the SEC website at www.sec.gov, then click on "Filings & Forms (EDGAR)."
Describe what you find there and discuss why this is a valuable service to companies
and investors.**

As stated on the SEC's website, EDGAR, the Electronic Data Gathering, Analysis, and Retrieval system, performs automated collection, validation, indexing, acceptance, and forwarding of submissions by companies and others who are required by law to file forms with the U.S. Securities and Exchange Commission (SEC). Its primary purpose is to increase the efficiency and fairness of the securities market for the benefit of investors, corporations, and the economy by accelerating the receipt, acceptance, dissemination, and analysis of time-sensitive corporate information filed with the agency.

In short, the system helps companies by distributing this information for them and reducing the burden of making the information available to the public. For the investor it offers a single place to explore the financial documents filed by public corporations, insurance companies, and mutual funds.

Chapter 9
Marketing Concepts and Strategies

Learning Objectives
After reading this chapter, you should be able to:

1. Explain what marketing is.
2. Describe the four utilities created by marketing.
3. Explain how techniques such as social commerce and permission-based marketing help companies nurture positive customer relationships.
4. Explain why and how companies learn about their customers.
5. Discuss how marketing research helps the marketing effort and highlight its limitations.
6. Outline the three steps in the strategic marketing planning process.
7. Define market segmentation and name three fundamental factors used to identify segments.
8. Identify the four elements of a company's marketing mix.

True-False
Indicate whether the statement is generally true or false by placing a "T" or an "F" in the space provided. If it is a false statement, correct it so that it becomes a true statement.

_____ 1. Marketing applies to goods, services, nonprofit organizations, people, places, and causes.

_____ 2. Place marketing promotes a cause or a social issue—such as physical fitness, cancer awareness, recycling, or highway safety—while also promoting a company and its products.

_____ 3. Marketing plays an important role in society by helping people satisfy their needs and wants and by helping organizations determine what to produce.

_____ 4. The exchange process occurs when a consumer or organization trades something of value (usually money) for something else of value.

_____ 5. Utility is any attribute that increases the value that customers place on the product.

_____ 6. The marketing concept suggests that companies should be focused more on their own production or sales functions and less on long-term relationships with markets and customers.

_____ 7. Relationship marketing is the degree to which customers continue to buy from a particular retailer or buy the products offered by a particular manufacturer.

_____ 8. The product concept emphasizes building a business by generating as many sales transactions as possible, rather than on creating lasting relationships with customers.

_____ 9. Stealth marketing refers to practices in which customers are unaware that a company is marketing to them.

_____ 10. The consumer market is composed of both companies and a variety of noncommercial institutions, from local school districts to the federal government.

_____ 11. Cognitive dissonance occurs when our beliefs and behaviors do not match.

_____ 12. Most organizational purchases are carefully evaluated for financial impact, technical compatibility, reliability, and other objective factors.

_____ 13. Marketing research can provide the answer to every strategic or tactical question.

_____ 14. Market segments are homogeneous groups of customers that are significantly different from each other.

_____ 15. Undifferentiated marketing requires substantial resources to tailor products, prices, promotional efforts, and distribution arrangements for each customer group.

_____ 16. Concentrated marketing refers to the process of designing a company's offerings, messages, and operating policies so that both the company and its products occupy distinct and desirable competitive positions in the target customers' minds.

_____ 17. From a marketing standpoint, a product is anything offered for the purpose of satisfying a want or a need in a marketing exchange, including the product itself plus brand name, design, packaging, services, quality, and warranty.

_____ 18. A product mix is a group of similar products from a single company.

_____ 19. The terms _marketing channels_, _marketing intermediaries_, and _distribution channels_ are used interchangeably by marketers.

_____ 20. The goals of promotion include informing, persuading, and reminding.

Multiple Choice
Circle the best answer for each of the following questions.

1. Which of the following is true about marketing?
    a. It is planning and executing the conception, pricing, promotion, and distribution of ideas, goods, and services to create exchanges that satisfy individual and organizational objectives
    b. It involves all the decisions related to a product's characteristics, price, production specifications, market-entry data, distribution, promotion, and sales
    c. It involves understanding customers' needs and their buying behavior, creating consumer awareness, providing customer service, and maintaining relationships with customers after the sales transaction is complete
    d. All of the above

2. A need can be described as:
    a. Any time there is a difference or a gap between a consumer's actual state and ideal state.
    b. Demand created by the marketplace.
    c. Specific wants of a consumer or company.
    d. All of the above

3. Form utility:
    a. Occurs when organizations make products available where consumers want to buy them.
    b. Occurs when organizations change raw materials into finished goods desired by consumers.
    c. Occurs when organizations make products available when consumers want to buy them.
    d. Is the satisfaction that buyers get when they actually possess a product, both legally and physically.

4. All of the following are results of satisfying and delighting your customers except:
    a. Greater customer loyalty, which can sharply reduce marketing costs
    b. Positive word of mouth, in which happy customers help promote your products to friends, family, and colleagues
    c. An increased sensitivity to price
    d. The opportunity to sell different types of products to customers who are satisfied with the purchases they have made from you already

5. When customers create and share information about products, by facilitating the exchange of information in ways that promote positive buying responses, this is known as:
    a. Social networking
    b. E-commerce
    c. Social commerce
    d. Social responsibility

6. Which of the following is a step in the classical consumer buying process?
   a. Recognizing a need
   b. Gathering information
   c. Identifying alternative solutions
   d. All of the above

7. Which of the following is a way that culture can shape a consumer's purchasing decisions?
   a. By shaping their values, attitudes, and beliefs, and influencing the way they respond to the world around them
   b. By providing information about product choices and establishing values that individual consumers perceive as important
   c. By encouraging them to express their identity through their purchases by emphasizing the image value of goods and services
   d. None of the above

8. Which is a way in which organizational purchasing differs from consumer purchasing?
   a. Purchases tend to be spontaneous
   b. There is a closer relationship between buyer and seller
   c. There are fewer people involved
   d. The process is less formal

9. Database marketing is:
   a. The process of recording and analyzing customer interactions, preferences, and buying behavior for the purpose of contacting and transacting with customers
   b. The videotaping of shoppers so that researchers can study their movements and behaviors throughout a store
   c. The process of gathering and analyzing market intelligence about customers, markets, and related marketing issues
   d. All of the above

10. The first step in strategic marketing planning is:
    a. Assessing marketing opportunities and setting objectives
    b. Dividing the market into segments, choosing target markets and the position to be established in those markets, and then developing a marketing mix
    c. Examining the current marketing situation by reviewing past performance, evaluating competition, examining internal strengths and weaknesses, and analyzing the external environment
    d. None of the above

11. Market penetration refers to:
    a. Creating new products for your current markets
    b. Selling more of your existing products in current markets
    c. Selling your existing products to new markets
    d. Creating new products for new markets

12. Which of the following is not considered to be a company's external environment:
    a. Technology
    b. Laws and regulations
    c. Customers
    d. The natural environment

13. Psychographics are:
    a. Characteristics such as age, gender, income, race, occupation, and ethnic group
    b. Customers' knowledge of, attitude toward, use of, or response to products or product characteristics
    c. Geographical units such as regions, cities, counties, or neighborhoods that allow companies to customize and sell products that meet the needs of specific markets
    d. The analysis of people from the inside, focusing on their psychological makeup, including attitudes, interests, opinions, and lifestyles

14. Which of the following best describes the differentiated marketing strategy?
    a. It ignores differences among buyers and offers only one product or product line to satisfy the entire market
    b. It offers a variety of products to several target customer groups
    c. It acknowledges that other market segments may exist but chooses to target just one
    d. It concludes that all buyers have similar needs that can be served with the same standardized product

15. Which of the following is not a primary element of the marketing mix?
    a. Price
    b. Distribution
    c. Advertising
    d. Product

16. The four stages of the product lifecycle are:
    a. Introduction, growth, maturity, and decline
    b. Interest, attention, preference, and purchase
    c. Development, manufacture, distribution, and service
    d. None of the above

17. A number of factors influence pricing decisions, including:
    a. Marketing objectives and government regulations
    b. Production costs and customer perceptions
    c. Competition and customer demand
    d. All of the above

18. Which of the following statements best describes the cost-plus pricing strategy?
    a. Pricing a hot new product at a temporarily high level to capture demand from the first wave of buyers
    b. Setting the price high to convey the notion of quality and exclusivity
    c. Adding a given profit margin to the company's cost of creating or buying the product to yield a sales price
    d. Setting the price low in order to penetrate a market

19. Which of the following is not considered a type of promotional activity?
    a. Advertising
    b. Public relations
    c. Distribution
    d. Direct selling

Match the Terms and Concepts with Their Definitions

A. behavioral segmentation
B. cause-related marketing
C. cognitive dissonance
D. consumer market
E. customer buying behavior
F. customer loyalty
G. customer service
H. database marketing
I. demographics
J. distribution channels
K. exchange process
L. form utility
M. geodemographics
N. geographic segmentation
O. market
P. market segmentation
Q. market share
R. marketing
S. marketing concept
T. marketing mix
U. marketing research

V. marketing strategy
W. need
X. organizational market
Y. permission-based marketing
Z. place marketing
AA. place utility
BB. positioning
CC. possession utility
DD. price
EE. product
FF. promotion
GG. psychographics
HH. relationship marketing
II. social commerce
JJ. stealth marketing
KK. strategic marketing planning
LL. target markets
MM. time utility
NN. transaction
OO. utility
PP. wants

119

_____ 1. Process of planning and executing the conception, pricing, promotion, and distribution of ideas, goods, and services to create and maintain relationships

_____ 2. Efforts a company makes to satisfy its customers to help them realize the greatest possible value from the products they are purchasing

_____ 3. Marketing efforts to attract people and organizations to a particular geographical area

_____ 4. Identification and marketing of a social issue, cause, or idea to selected target markets

_____ 5. Difference between a person's actual state and his or her ideal state; provides the basic motivation to make a purchase

_____ 6. Specific goods, services, experiences, or other entities that are desirable in light of a person's experiences, culture, and personality

_____ 7. Act of obtaining a desired object or service from another party by offering something of value in return

_____ 8. Exchange of value between parties

_____ 9. A group of customers who need or want a particular product and have the money to buy it

_____ 10. Customer value created by converting raw materials and other inputs into finished goods and services

_____ 11. Customer value added by making a product available at a convenient time

_____ 12. Customer value added by making a product available in a convenient location

_____ 13. Customer value created when someone takes ownership of a product

_____ 14. Approach to business management that stresses customer needs and wants, seeks long-term profitability, and integrates marketing with other functional units within the organization

_____ 15. A focus on developing and maintaining long-term relationships with customers, suppliers, and distribution partners for mutual benefit

_____ 16. Degree to which customers continue to buy from a particular retailer or buy the products of a particular manufacturer or service provider

_____17. The creation and sharing of product-related information among customers and potential customers

_____18. Marketing approach in which firms first ask permission to deliver messages to an audience and then promise to restrict their communication efforts to those subject areas in which audience members have expressed interest

_____19. The delivery of marketing messages to people who are not aware that they are being marketed to; these messages can be delivered by either acquaintances or strangers, depending on the technique

_____20. Individuals or households that buy goods and services for personal use

_____21. Businesses, nonprofit organizations, and government agencies that purchase goods and services for use in their operations

_____22. Behavior exhibited by consumers as they consider, select, and purchase goods and services

_____23. Tension that exists when a person's beliefs don't match his or her behaviors; a common example is buyer's remorse, when someone regrets a purchase immediately after making it

_____24. The collection and analysis of information for making marketing decisions

_____25. Process of building, maintaining, and using customer databases for the purpose of contacting customers and transacting business

_____26. The process of examining an organization's current marketing situation, assessing opportunities and setting objectives, then developing a marketing strategy to reach those objectives

_____27. A firm's portion of the total sales in a market

_____28. Overall plan for marketing a product; includes the identification of target market segments, a positioning strategy, and a marketing mix

_____29. Power of a good or service to satisfy a human need

_____30. Division of a diverse market into smaller, relatively homogeneous groups with similar needs, wants, and purchase behaviors

_____31. Study of statistical characteristics of a population

_____32. Classification of customers on the basis of their psychological makeup, interests, and lifestyles

_____33. Categorization of customers according to their relationship with products or response to product characteristics

_____34. Good or service used as the basis of commerce

_____35. Method of combining geographical data with demographic data to develop profiles of neighborhood segments

_____36. Specific customer groups or segments to whom a company wants to sell a particular product

_____37. Using promotion, product, distribution, and price to differentiate a good or service from those of competitors in the mind of the prospective buyer

_____38. The four key elements of marketing strategy: product, price, distribution, and promotion

_____39. Categorization of customers according to their geographical location

_____40. The amount of money charged for a product or service

_____41. Systems for moving goods and services from producers to customers; also known as marketing channels

_____42. Wide variety of persuasive techniques used by companies to communicate with their target markets and the general public

Learning Objectives—Short Answer or Essay Questions

1. Explain what marketing is.

2. Describe the four utilities created by marketing.

3. Explain how techniques such as social commerce and permission-based marketing help companies nurture positive customer relationships.

4. Explain why and how companies learn about their customers.

5. Discuss how marketing research helps the marketing effort and highlight its limitations.

6. Outline the three steps in the strategic marketing planning process.

7. Define market segmentation and name three fundamental factors used to identify segments.

8. Identify the four elements of a company's marketing mix.

Critical Thinking Questions

1. Explain the marketing concept and compare it to the sales and production concepts.

2. Compare and contrast the undifferentiated, differentiated, and concentrated marketing strategies.

3. Discuss the concept of product identity.

True-False—Answers

1. True	8. False	15. False
2. False	9. True	16. False
3. True	10. False	17. True
4. True	11. True	18. False
5. True	12. True	19. True
6. False	13. False	20. False
7. False	14. True	

Multiple Choice—Answers

1.	D	8.	B	15.	C
2.	A	9.	A	16.	A
3.	B	10.	C	17.	D
4.	C	11.	B	18.	C
5.	C	12.	C	19.	C
6.	D	13.	D		
7.	A	14.	B		

Match the Terms and Concepts with Their Definitions – Answers

1.	R	15.	HH	29.	OO
2.	G	16.	F	30.	P
3.	Z	17.	II	31.	I
4.	B	18.	Y	32.	GG
5.	W	19.	JJ	33.	A
6.	PP	20.	D	34.	EE
7.	K	21.	X	35.	M
8.	NN	22.	E	36.	LL
9.	O	23.	C	37.	BB
10.	L	24.	U	38.	T
11.	MM	25.	H	39.	N
12.	AA	26.	KK	40.	DD
13.	CC	27.	Q	41.	J
14.	S	28.	V	42.	FF

Learning Objectives—Short Answer or Essay Question - Answers

1. **Explain what marketing is.**

   Marketing is the process of planning and executing the conception, pricing, promotion, and distribution of ideas, goods, and services to create exchanges that satisfy individual and organizational objectives. It involves all decisions related to a product's characteristics, price, production specifications, market-entry date, distribution, promotion, and sale. It involves understanding and satisfying customers' needs and buying behavior to encourage consumer purchases, in addition to maintaining long-term relationships with customers after the sale.

2. **Describe four utilities created by marketing.**

   Marketers enhance the appeal of their products and services by adding utility. Form utility is created when companies turn raw materials into finished goods desired by consumers. Time utility is created by making the product available when the consumer wants to buy it. Place utility is created when a product is made available at a location that is convenient for the consumer. Possession utility is created by facilitating the transfer of ownership from seller to buyer.

3. **Explain how techniques such as social commerce and permission-based marketing help companies nurture positive customer relationships.**

   Social commerce is an important new way for customers to participate in the marketing process, which helps shift the relationship power from sellers to buyers. Permission-based marketing helps in the effort to build long-term relationships by demonstrating not only respect for customers but a willingness to meet *their* needs, as opposed to the marketer's need.

4. **Explain why and how companies learn about their customers.**

Today's customers generally are sophisticated, price sensitive, demanding, more impatient, more informed, and difficult to satisfy. Companies learn about their customers so they can stay in touch with their current needs and wants, deliver quality products, and provide effective customer service. Such attention tends to keep customers satisfied and helps retain their long-term loyalty. Moreover, studies show that sales to repeat customers are more profitable. Most companies learn about their customers by studying consumer buying behavior, conducting marketing research, and capturing and analyzing customer data.

5. **Discuss how marketing research helps the marketing effort, and highlight its limitations.**

Marketing research can help companies set goals, develop new products, segment markets, plan future marketing programs, evaluate the effectiveness of a marketing program, keep an eye on competition, and measure customer satisfaction. On the other hand, marketing research is a poor predictor of what will excite consumers in the future. It is sometimes ineffective because it is conducted in an artificial setting. And, it is not a substitute for good judgment.

6. **Outline the three steps in the strategic marketing planning process.**

The three steps in the strategic marketing planning process are (1) examining your current marketing situation, which includes reviewing your past performance, evaluating your competition, examining your internal strengths and weaknesses, and analyzing the external environment; (2) assessing your opportunities and setting your objectives; and (3) developing your marketing strategy, which covers segmenting your market, choosing your target markets, positioning your product, and creating a marketing mix to satisfy the target market.

7. **Define market segmentation, and name three fundamental factors commonly used to identify segments.**

Market segmentation is the process of subdividing a market into homogeneous groups to identify potential customers and to devise marketing approaches geared to their needs and interests. The three primary factors used to identify segments are demographics (external statistical descriptors such as age, income, gender, and profession), psychographics (internal descriptors such as attitudes, interests, and values, as well as behaviors and habits), and geographics (location).

8. **Identify the four elements of a company's marketing mix.**

The four elements are product, price, distribution, and customer communication. Products are goods, services, persons, places, ideas, organizations, or anything else offered for the purpose of satisfying a want or need in a marketing exchange. Price is the amount of money customers pay for the product. Distribution is the organized network of firms that move the goods and services from the producer to the customer. Customer communication involves the activities used to communicate with and promote products to target markets.

Critical Thinking Questions - Answers

1. **Explain the marketing concept and compare it to the sales and production concepts.**

    In earlier business eras, companies typically focused more on their own production (production concept) or sales functions (sales concept) and less on long-term relationships with markets and customers. In contrast, many of today's companies try to embrace the marketing concept, the idea that companies should respond to customers' needs and wants while seeking long-term profitability and coordinating their own marketing efforts to achieve the company's long-term goals. These customer-focused companies build their marketing strategies around the goal of long-term relationships with satisfied customers. The term *relationship marketing* is often applied to these efforts to distinguish them from efforts that emphasize production or sales transactions. One of the most significant goals of relationship marketing is customer loyalty, the degree to which customers continue to buy from a particular retailer or buy the products offered by a particular manufacturer. The payoff from becoming customer-focused can be considerable, but the process of transforming a product- or sales-driven company into one that embraces the marketing concept can take years and involve changes to major systems and processes throughout the company, as well as the basic culture of the company itself.

    The production concept focuses on product features and quality, rather than working backwards from customers to create solutions that meet their needs and wants, and is a risky strategy. The sales concept emphasizes building a business by generating as many sales transactions as possible, rather than on creating lasting relationships with customers.

2. **Compare and contrast the undifferentiated, differentiated, and concentrated marketing strategies.**

    Companies that practice undifferentiated marketing (or mass marketing) ignore differences among buyers and offer only one product or product line to satisfy the entire market. This strategy, which concludes that all buyers have similar needs that can be served with the same standardized product, was more popular in the past than it is today.

    By contrast, companies that manufacture or sell a variety of products to several target customer groups practice differentiated marketing. Differentiated marketing is a popular strategy, but it requires substantial resources because you have to tailor products, prices, promotional efforts, and distribution arrangements for each customer group.

Concentrated marketing is the narrowest approach, focusing on only a single market segment. With this approach, you acknowledge that various other market segments may exist but you choose to target just one. The biggest advantage of concentrated marketing is that it allows you to focus all your time and resources on a single type of customer (which is why this approach is usually the best option for startup companies, by the way). The strategy can be risky, however, because you've staked your fortunes on just one segment.

3.   Discuss the concept of product identity.

In all but the most basic commodities, companies work hard to establish unique identities for their goods and services. The essential element of product identity is the brand, which is a unique name, symbol, or design that sets a product (or an entire company) apart from its competitors. Brand names and symbols can be given protected legal status as trademarks, which prevents other companies from using them. Above and beyond the functional value of the product, the brand itself has value as well, a concept known as brand equity. Over time, every brand takes on a particular meaning – positive or negative – in the eyes of customers.

Chapter 10
Products and Pricing

Learning Objectives
After reading this chapter, you should be able to:

1. Describe the four stages in the life cycle of a product.
2. Describe six stages of product development.
3. Cite three levels of brand loyalty.
4. Discuss the functions of packaging and labeling.
5. Identify four ways of expanding a product line and discuss two risks that product-line extensions pose.
6. List the factors that influence pricing decisions and identify seven common pricing strategies.
7. Explain why cost-based pricing can be a flawed strategy.

True-False
Indicate whether the statement is generally true or false by placing a "T" or an "F" in the space provided. If it is a false statement, correct it so that it becomes a true statement.

_____ 1. The product continuum indicates the relative amounts of tangible and intangible components in a product.

_____ 2. Capital items are relatively inexpensive goods and services that organizations generally use within a year of purchase.

_____ 3. The concept of product life cycle suggests that products pass through four distinct stages in sales and profits.

_____ 4. When a product reaches the decline phase of the product life cycle, the company must decide whether to keep it and reduce the product's costs to compensate for declining sales or discontinue it and focus on developing newer products.

_____ 5. Idea screening is the first step in the product development process, and its purpose is to come up with ideas that will satisfy unmet needs.

_____ 6. During prototype development, a firm introduces the product in selected areas of the country and monitors consumer reactions.

_____ 7. Branding helps a company by providing customers with a way of recognizing and specifying a particular product so that they can choose it again or recommend it to others.

_____ 8. The notion of the value of a brand is also called brand loyalty.

_____ 9. Co-branding occurs when two or more companies team up to closely link their names in a single product.

_____ 10. A product line is group of products from a single manufacturer that are similar in terms of use or characteristics.

_____ 11. Expanding a product line by adding new and similar products with the same product name is a strategy known as family branding.

_____ 12. There are no limits to how far a brand name can be stretched to accommodate new products and still fit the buyer's perception of what the brand stands for.

_____ 13. Pricing decisions for a product are determined by manufacturing and selling costs only.

_____ 14. It can be said that a company's costs establish a ceiling for prices, and demand for a product establishes a floor.

_____ 15. The penetration pricing concept is used to build sales volume by charging a low initial price.

_____ 16. Loss-leader pricing sets a price on one product so low that they lose money on every sale while recouping that loss by enticing customers to try a new product or to buy other products.

Multiple Choice

Circle the best answer for each of the following questions.

1. Which of the following best describes a convenience product?
   a. Goods and services that people buy less frequently, such as music players, computers, refrigerators, and college educations
   b. Particular brands that the buyer especially wants and will seek out, regardless of location or price
   c. Goods and services that people buy frequently, usually without much conscious planning
   d. Products that many people do not normally think of buying, such as life insurance, cemetery plots, and new products

2. Which of the following are examples of industrial products that are classified as installations?
   a. Factories, power plants, airports, production lines, and semiconductor fabrication machinery
   b. Pencils, nails, and light bulbs
   c. Desks, telephones, and fax machines
   d. Iron ore, crude petroleum, lumber, and chemicals

3. Which statement most accurately describes the growth phase of the product lifecycle?
   a. It extends from the research-and-development phase through the product's first commercial availability
   b. It is marked by a rapid jump in sales and an increase in the number of competitors and distribution outlets
   c. It is usually the longest in the product lifecycle; total sales begin to level off or show a slight decline
   d. None of the above

4. All of the following are true about the maturity phase of the product lifecycle except:
   a. It is the longest in the product life cycle
   b. Competition begins to increase, as does the struggle for market share
   c. The only way a firm can expand its sales in this phase is to win sales away from other suppliers
   d. Most companies try to keep mature products alive so they can use the resulting profits to fund the development of new products

5. Which of the following are the steps in the product development process?
   a. Idea generation, idea screening, business analysis, prototype development, test marketing, and commercialization
   b. Recognizing a need, evaluating alternatives, selecting the best alternative
   c. Idea generation, idea screening, business analysis, prototype development, test marketing, and product launch
   d. Both a and c

6. The notion of a brand can be described as:
   a. A unique name, symbol, or design that sets the product apart from those offered by competitors
   b. The legal protections afforded by a trademark and any relevant intellectual property
   c. The overall company or organizational brand
   d. All of the above

7. Select the statement that best describes the concept of brand preference.
    a. People will purchase the product if it is available, although they may still be willing to experiment with alternatives
    b. Buyers will accept no substitute
    c. People are likely to buy a product because they are familiar with it
    d. All of the above

8. Which statement best describes a private brand?
    a. A brand offered and promoted by a national manufacturer
    b. A product packaged in plain containers that bears only the name of the product
    c. A brand not linked to a manufacturer but instead carrying a wholesaler's or a retailer's brand
    d. None of the above

9. Packaging contributes to the product in all of the following ways except:
    a. It protects products from damage or tampering
    b. It can make it convenient for customers to purchase or use a product
    c. It can be an essential part of the product itself
    d. All of the above

10. Which of the following terms is not synonymous with brand manager?
    a. Product manager
    b. Product line manger
    c. Marketing manager
    d. All of the above

11. Which of the following best describes the concept of product mix depth?
    a. It has several different product lines within it
    b. It has a number of versions of *each* product in a product line
    c. It carries several items in each of its product lines
    d. None of the above

12. A brand extension occurs when:
    a. A company adds new and similar products with the same product name
    b. A company applies a successful brand name to a new product category
    c. Both a and b
    d. None of the above

13. Which of the following is a limitation of product line extension?
    a. Diluting the brand's meaning in the minds of target customers by stretching it to cover too many categories or types
    b. New products can cannibalize, or take sales away from, their existing products
    c. Both a and b
    d. None of the above

14. Which of the following is a factor in product pricing?
    a. Marketing objectives
    b. Government regulations
    c. Consumer perceptions
    d. All of the above

15. Which statement best describes the concept of price fixing?
    a. An agreement among two or more companies supplying the same type of products as to the prices they will charge
    b. The practice of unfairly offering attractive discounts to some customers but not to others
    c. Pricing schemes that are considered misleading
    d. All of the above

16. Which of the following statements refers to the concept of optimal pricing?
    a. Using computer software to generate the ideal price for every item
    b. Setting the price high during a product's introductory phase
    c. Adding a markup to the cost of the product
    d. Charging a fairly affordable price for a high-quality offering

17. Setting prices low for a product's introductory phase is known as:
    a. Skim pricing
    b. Penetration pricing
    c. Predatory pricing
    d. Value pricing

18. Which of the following is not a type of price adjustment strategy?
    a. Price discounts
    b. Bundling
    c. Dynamic pricing
    d. Loss-leader pricing

Match the Terms and Concepts with Their Definitions

A.	auction	M.	commercialization
B.	brand	N.	discount pricing
C.	brand equity	O.	dynamic pricing
D.	brand extension	P.	family branding
E.	brand loyalty	Q.	fixed costs
F.	brand manager	R.	generic products
G.	brand mark	S.	license
H.	brand names	T.	loss-leader pricing
I.	break-even analysis	U.	national brands
J.	break-even point	V.	penetration pricing
K.	bundling	W.	price elasticity
L.	co-branding	X.	private brands

Y.   product life cycle
Z.   product line
AA. product mix
BB. skim pricing

CC. test marketing
DD. trademarks
EE. Universal Product Codes (UPCs)
FF. variable costs

_____ 1. Four basic stages through which a product progresses: introduction, growth, maturity, and decline

_____ 2. Product-development stage in which a product is sold on a limited basis—a trial introduction

_____ 3. Large-scale production and distribution of a product

_____ 4. Complete list of all products that a company offers for sale

_____ 5. The value that a company has built up in a brand

_____ 6. The degree to which customers continue to purchase a specific brand

_____ 7. Portion of a brand that can be expressed orally, including letters, words, or numbers

_____ 8. Portion of a brand that cannot be expressed verbally

_____ 9. Brands that have been given legal protection so that their owners have exclusive rights to their use

_____ 10. Brands owned by the manufacturers and distributed nationally

_____ 11. Brands that carry the label of a retailer or a wholesaler rather than a manufacturer

_____ 12. Products characterized by a plain label, with no advertising and no brand name

_____ 13. Partnership between two or more companies to closely link their brand names together for a single product

_____ 14. Agreement to produce and market another company's product in exchange for a royalty or fee

_____ 15. A bar code on a product's package that provides information read by optical scanners

_____ 16. The person who develops and implements a complete strategy and marketing program for a specific product or brand

_____ 17. A series of related products offered by a firm

_____ 18. A name, term, sign, symbol, design, or combination of those used to identify the products of a firm and to differentiate them from competing products

_____ 19. Using a brand name on a variety of related products

_____ 20. Applying a successful brand name to a new product category

_____ 21. A measure of the sensitivity of demand to changes in price

_____ 22. Method of calculating the minimum volume of sales needed at a given price to cover all costs

_____ 23. Business costs that increase with the number of units produced

_____ 24. Business costs that remain constant regardless of the number of units produced

_____ 25. Sales volume at a given price that will cover all of a company's costs

_____ 26. Charging a high price for a new product during the introductory stage and lowering the price later

_____ 27. Introducing a new product at a low price in hopes of building sales volume quickly

_____ 28. Selling one product at a loss as a way to entice customers to consider other products

_____ 29. Selling method in which the price is set by customers bidding against each other

_____ 30. Offering a temporary reduction in price

_____ 31. Offering several products for a single price that is presumably lower than the total of the products' individual prices

_____ 32. Continually adjusting prices to reflect changes in supply and demand

Learning Objectives—Short Answer or Essay Questions

1. Describe the four stages in the life cycle of a product.

2. Describe six stages of product development.

3. Cite three levels of brand loyalty.

4. Discuss the functions of packaging and labeling.

5. Identify four ways of expanding a product line and discuss two risks that product-line extensions pose.

6. List the factors that influence pricing decisions and identify seven common pricing strategies.

7. Explain why cost-based pricing can be a flawed strategy.

Critical Thinking Questions

1. Discuss the four types of consumer products and cite examples of each.

2. List the six industrial product classifications and cite examples of each.

3. Discuss the role of government regulation in pricing and discuss three areas where such regulations come into play.

True-False—Answers

1. True	7. True	13. False
2. False	8. False	14. False
3. True	9. True	15. True
4. True	10. True	16. True
5. False	11. True	
6. False	12. False	

Multiple Choice—Answers

1. C	7. A	13. C
2. A	8. C	14. D
3. B	9. D	15. A
4. B	10. C	16. A
5. D	11. B	17. B
6. D	12. B	18. D

Match the Terms and Concepts with Their Definitions - Answers

1. Y	12. R	23. FF
2. CC	13. L	24. Q
3. M	14. S	25. J
4. AA	15. EE	26. BB
5. C	16. F	27. V
6. E	17. Z	28. T
7. H	18. B	29. A
8. G	19. P	30. N
9. DD	20. D	31. K
10. U	21. W	32. O
11. X	22. I	

Learning Objectives—Short Answer or Essay Question - Answers

1. **Describe the four stages in the life cycle of a product.**
Products start in the introductory stage, during which marketers focus on stimulating demand for the new product. As the product progresses through the growth stage, marketers focus on increasing the product's market share. During the maturity stage, marketers try to extend the life of the product by highlighting improvements or by repackaging the product in different sizes. Eventually, products move to a decline stage, where the marketer must decide whether to keep the product and reduce its costs to compensate for declining sales or to discontinue it.

2. **Describe six stages of product development.**
The first two stages of product development involve generating and screening ideas to isolate those with the most potential. In the third stage, promising ideas are analyzed to determine their likely profitability. Those that appear worthwhile enter the fourth, or prototype development stage, in which a limited number of the products are created. In the fifth stage, the product is test marketed to determine buyer response. Products that survive the testing process are then commercialized, the final stage.

3. **Cite three levels of brand loyalty.**
The first level of brand loyalty is brand awareness, in which the buyer is familiar with the product. The next level is brand preference, in which the buyer will select the product if it is available. The final level is brand insistence, in which the buyer will accept no substitute.

4. **Discuss the functions of packaging and labeling.**
Packaging provides protection for the product, makes products easier to display, and attracts attention. In addition, packaging enhances the convenience of the product and communicates its attributes to the buyer. Labels help identify and distinguish the brand

and product. They provide information about the product—including ingredients, risks, shelf life, and operating procedures. And they contain UPC codes, which are used for scanning sales information and monitoring inventory and pricing.

5. **Identify four ways of expanding a product line, and discuss two risks that product-line extensions pose.**
   A product line can be expanded by filling gaps in the market, extending the line to include new varieties of existing products, extending the brand to new product categories, and stretching the line to include lower- or higher-priced items. Two of the biggest risks with product-line extensions include a loss of brand identity (weakening of the brand's meaning), and cannibalization of sales of other products in the product line.

6. **List the factors that influence pricing decisions, and identify seven common pricing strategies.**
   Pricing decisions are influenced by manufacturing and selling costs, competition, the needs of wholesalers and retailers who distribute the product to the final customer, a firm's marketing objectives, government regulations, quality perceptions, and customer demand. Common pricing methods include cost-based pricing, price-based pricing, optimal pricing, skim pricing, penetration pricing, loss-leader pricing, and auction pricing.

7. **Explain why cost-based pricing can be a flawed strategy.**
   Cost-based pricing suffers from two major weaknesses. First, determining variable costs can be difficult since they often depend on production and sales volume. As the projected volume goes up or down, variable costs (necessary to compute the break-even point or profit margin) might be going down or up in response. Second, cost-based pricing doesn't take into account the influences of competitors or customers, both of which can dramatically affect the ability to sell at a given price point.

Critical Thinking Questions - Answers

1. Discuss the four types of consumer products and cite examples of each.

Consumer products can be classified into four subgroups, depending on how people shop for them:

- Convenience products are the goods and services that people buy frequently, usually without much conscious planning, such as toothpaste, dry cleaning, and gasoline.

- Shopping products are fairly important goods and services that people buy less frequently, such as music players, computers, refrigerators, and college educations. Such purchases require more thought and comparison shopping to check on price, features, quality, and reputation.

- Specialty products are particular brands that the buyer especially wants and will seek

141

out, regardless of location or price, such as Prada clothing and accessories or Suzuki violin lessons. Specialty products are not necessarily expensive, but they are products that customers go out of their way to buy and for which they rarely accept substitutes.

- <u>Unsought products</u> are products that many people do not normally think of buying, such as life insurance, cemetery plots, and new products. Part of the marketing challenge in these cases is simply making people aware of the product.

2. List the six industrial product classifications and cite examples of each.

- <u>Raw materials</u> such as iron ore, crude petroleum, lumber, and chemicals are used in the production of final products.

- <u>Components</u> such as semiconductors and fasteners are similar to raw materials; they also become part of the manufacturers' final products. Many companies also buy completed subsystems that they then assemble into final products; Boeing buys complete engines for its aircraft, for instance.

- <u>Supplies</u> such as pencils, nails, and light bulbs that are used in a firm's daily operations are considered expense items.

- <u>Installations</u> such as factories, power plants, airports, production lines, and semiconductor fabrication machinery are major capital projects.

- <u>Equipment</u> includes less-expensive capital items such as desks, telephones, and fax machines that are shorter lived than installations.

- <u>Business services</u> range from simple and fairly risk-free services such as landscaping and cleaning to complex services such as management consulting and auditing.

3. Discuss the role of government regulation in pricing and discuss three areas where such regulations come into play.

Government plays a big role in pricing. To protect consumers and encourage fair competition, governments around the world have enacted various price-related laws over the years. These regulations are particularly important in three areas: (1) price fixing—an agreement among two or more companies supplying the same type of products as to the prices they will charge, (2) price discrimination— an agreement among two or more companies supplying the same type of products as to the prices they will charge, and (3) deceptive pricing—pricing schemes that are considered misleading.

Chapter 11
Distribution and Customer Communication

Learning Objectives
After reading this chapter, you should be able to:

1. Explain what marketing intermediaries do and list their seven primary functions.
2. Explain how wholesalers and retailers function as intermediaries.
3. Discuss the key factors that influence channel design and selection.
4. Differentiate intensive, selective, and exclusive distribution strategies.
5. Identify the seven categories of customer communication.
6. Discuss the importance of integrated marketing communications.
7. Explain the purpose of defining a core marketing message.
8. Describe the use of social media in marketing communications.

True-False
Indicate whether the statement is generally true or false by placing a "T" or an "F" in the space provided. If it is a false statement, correct it so that it becomes a true statement.

_____ 1. Marketing channels are organized networks of systems and firms that work together to get goods and services from producer to customer.

_____ 2. Wholesalers known as drop shippers offer various levels of service from full-service firms that provide storage, sales, order processing, delivery, and promotional support.

_____ 3. The wheel of retailing describes a retailer's attempts to draw in more shoppers and increase the average revenue per customer by adding products unrelated to its original product mix.

_____ 4. Multichannel retailing refers to offering entertainment and education opportunities (such as cooking and home improvement classes) in addition to shopping.

_____ 5. Comparison shopping engines continue to evolve as tools to let consumers find the lowest prices.

_____ 6. E-commerce creates channel conflicts when manufacturers sell directly from their websites and compete with the retailers in their distribution mix.

_____ 7   Inventory control involves preparing orders for shipment and receiving orders when shipments arrive.

_____ 8.   Supporting customers is essential to ensuring customer satisfaction because it increases opportunities for repeat business from existing customers and referrals to new customers.

_____ 9.   The message is the single most important idea that a company hopes to convey to the target audience about its product.

_____ 10.   It is not possible for a company to use the push marketing strategy and the pull marketing strategy simultaneously.

_____ 11.   Sales follow-up refers to checking with the customer after a sale to make sure everything is satisfactory and to build goodwill in anticipation of future sales opportunities.

_____ 12.   Institutional advertising promotes specific goods and services.

_____ 13.   Product placement occurs when an advertiser puts its products right into a TV show or movie.

_____ 14.   Consumer promotion is aimed directly at final users of the product to stimulate repeat purchases and to entice new users.

_____ 15.   To protect the long-term value of their brands, advertisers need to seek a balance between effectiveness and sensitivity to their audiences.

Multiple Choice

Circle the best answer for each of the following questions.

1. Which of the following is not a function of a wholesaler?
    a. Selling products to consumers for personal use
    b. Matching buyers and sellers
    c. Gathering an assortment of goods
    d. Providing market information

2. Which of the following statements best describes a manufacturer's representative?
    a. They sell primarily to other intermediaries
    b. They sell various noncompeting product lines to business customers
    c. They are generally paid a commission for arranging sales
    d. Both b and c

3. A specialty store can be defined as:
   a. A supersized store that dominates a particular product category by stocking every conceivable variety of merchandise in every important product line in that category
   b. A store that carries only particular types of goods
   c. The classic major retailers in the United States that carry clothing, housewares, bedding, and furniture
   d. A store that tends to be fairly large with a wide variety of aggressively priced merchandise

4. Which of the following is not considered a type of nonstore retailing?
   a. Vending machines
   b. Mail order catalogs
   c. E-commerce websites
   d. None of the above

5. Which of the following is not a factor in determining a products distribution mix?
   a. Channel depth
   b. Channel length
   c. Market coverage
   d. Channel conflict

6. Which of the following best describes the concept of selective distribution?
   a. Products are made available in as many outlets as possible
   b. Products are offered in only one outlet in each market area
   c. Products are sold through a limited number of outlets that can give the product adequate sales and service support
   d. None of the above

7. Which of the following is not a step in the physical distribution process?
   a. Order processing
   b. Quality control
   c. Inventory control
   d. Warehousing

8. Communication strategy must identify:
   a. Communication goals
   b. Core message
   c. Market approach
   d. All of the above

9. Which of the following is not a goal of promotion?
   a. To persuade customers
   b. To entertain customers
   c. To remind customers
   d. To inform customers

10. Which of the following best describes the push marketing approach?
    a. Making a claim based on a rational argument supported by solid evidence
    b. Appealing to an audience's feelings and sympathies
    c. A producer focusing its marketing efforts on its intermediaries
    d. A producer focusing its marketing efforts on the end consumer

11. Which of the following would not be considered part of a company's communications mix?
    a. Pricing strategy
    b. Personal selling
    c. Advertising
    d. Direct marketing

12. Which of the following statements best describes sales prospecting?
    a. Considering various options for approaching a customer and preparing for the sales call
    b. Finding and qualifying potential buyers of the product or service
    c. Seeking to understand any questions or concerns the buyer might raise and providing information to address those issues
    d. Asking a prospective customer to buy the product

13. All of the following are types of advertising media except:
    a. Company brochures
    b. Television
    c. Newspapers
    d. Radio

14. Which of the following is a type of online advertising?
    a. Search engine advertising
    b. Online display advertising
    c. Direct email
    d. Both a and b

15. Direct marketing seeks to achieve which of the following?
    a. A response in the form of an order
    b. A request for further information
    c. A visit to a store or other place of business for purchase of a specific product or service
    d. All of the above

16. The wide variety of nonsales communications that businesses have with their many stakeholders—communities, investors, industry analysts, government agencies and officials, and the news media—is known as:
    a. Trade promotion
    b. Cross promotion
    c. Public relations
    d. Specialty advertising

17. Interactive venues such as blogs, wikis, podcasts, and social networking sites are types of:
    a. Specialty media
    b. Social media
    c. Word-of-mouth media
    d. None of the above

Match the Terms and Concepts with Their Definitions

A. advertising
B. category killers
C. channel conflict
D. communication mix
E. consumer promotion
F. coupons
G. department stores
H. direct mail
I. direct marketing
J. discount stores
K. distribution centers
L. distribution channels
M. distribution mix
N. distribution strategy
O. e-commerce
P. exclusive distribution
Q. institutional advertising
R. integrated marketing communications (IMC)
S. intensive distribution
T. logistics
U. mail-order firms
V. marketing intermediaries
W. materials handling
X. media
Y. merchant wholesalers
Z. multichannel retailing

AA. news conference
BB. news release
CC. online display advertising
DD. permission marketing
EE. personal selling
FF. persuasive advertising
GG. physical distribution
HH. point-of-purchase (POP) display
II. premiums
JJ. product advertising
KK. promotional strategy
LL. public relations
MM. pull strategy
NN. push strategy
OO. rebates
PP. reminder advertising
QQ. retail theater
RR. retailers
SS. sales promotion
TT. scrambled merchandising
UU. search advertising
VV. selective distribution
WW. social media
XX. specialty advertising
YY. specialty store
ZZ. telemarketing
AAA. trade allowance

BBB. trade promotions   EEE. wholesalers
CCC. warehouse   FFF. widgets
DDD. wheel of retailing   GGG. word of mouth

_____ 1.   Small software programs that provide part of the functionality of a website

_____ 2.   Organized networks of systems and firms that work together to get goods and
           services from producer to customer

_____ 3.   Firm's overall plan for moving products to intermediaries and final customers

_____ 4.   Businesspeople and organizations that channel goods and services from
           producers to customers

_____ 5.   Firms that sell products to other firms for resale or for organizational use

_____ 6.   Firms that sell goods and services to individuals for their own use rather than
           for resale

_____ 7.   Independent wholesalers that take legal title to goods they distribute

_____ 8.   Evolutionary process by which stores that feature low prices gradually
           upgrade until they no longer appeal to price-sensitive shoppers and are
           replaced by new low-price competitors

_____ 9.   Strategy of adding products unrelated to a store's original product mix

_____ 10. Store that carries only a particular type of goods

_____ 11. Discount chains that sell only one category of products

_____ 12. Full-price retailers that sell clothing, housewares, furniture, and related items

_____ 13. Retailers that sell a variety of goods below the market price by keeping their
           overhead low

_____ 14. Short for electronic commerce; retailing through the Internet and other
           electronic channels such as mobile phone services

_____ 15. Offering entertainment and education opportunities in addition to shopping

_____ 16. Coordinated efforts to reach customers through more than one retail channel

_____ 17. Companies that sell products through catalogs and ship them directly to customers

_____ 18. Combination of intermediaries and channels a producer uses to get a product to final customers

_____ 19. Market coverage strategy that tries to place a product in as many outlets as possible

_____ 20. Market coverage strategy that uses a limited number of outlets to distribute products

_____ 21. Market coverage strategy that gives intermediaries exclusive rights to sell a product in a specific geographical area

_____ 22. Disagreements between channel partners over pricing, product availability, and other distribution matters

_____ 23. All the activities required to move finished products from the producer to the customer

_____ 24. The planning, movement, and flow of goods and related information throughout the supply chain

_____ 25. Facility for storing inventory

_____ 26. Warehouse facilities that specialize in collecting and shipping merchandise

_____ 27. Movement of goods within a firm's warehouse terminal, factory, or store

_____ 28. Statement or document that defines the direction and scope of the promotional activities that a company will use to meet its marketing objectives

_____ 29. Advertising designed to encourage customers to try new products or to switch brands

_____ 30. Advertising intended to remind existing customers of a product's availability and benefits

_____ 31. Direct communication other than personal sales contacts designed to effect a measurable response

_____ 32. Promotional strategy that stimulates consumer demand, which then exerts pressure on wholesalers and retailers to carry a product

_____ 33.   Particular blend of personal selling, advertising, direct marketing, sales promotion, and public relations that a company uses to reach potential customers

_____ 34.   Strategy of coordinating and integrating all communications and promotional efforts with customers to ensure greater efficiency and effectiveness

_____ 35.   Personal communication between a seller and one or more potential buyers

_____ 36.   Paid, nonpersonal communication to a target market from an identified sponsor using mass communications channels

_____ 37.   Communications channels, such as newspapers, radio, and television

_____ 38.   Advertising that tries to sell specific goods or services, generally by describing features, benefits, and, occasionally, price

_____ 39.   Advertising that seeks to create goodwill and to build a desired image for a company rather than to sell specific products

_____ 40.   Online ads that are linked to search-engine results or website content

_____ 41.   Larger visual and multimedia ads that appear on websites

_____ 42.   Promotional approach designed to motivate wholesalers and retailers to push a producer's products to end users

_____ 43.   Advertising sent directly to potential customers, usually through the mail

_____ 44.   Promotional campaigns that send information only to those people who have specifically asked to receive it

_____ 45.   Selling or supporting the sales process over the telephone

_____ 46.   Wide range of events and activities (including coupons, rebates, contests, in-store demonstrations, free samples, trade shows, and point-of-purchase displays) designed to stimulate interest in a product

_____ 47.   Sales promotion aimed at final consumers

_____ 48.   Certificates that offer discounts on particular items and are redeemed at the time of purchase

_____ 49.   Post-sales reductions in price; must be applied for by the purchaser

_____ 50.   Advertising or other display materials set up at retail locations to promote products to potential customers as they are making their purchase decisions

_____ 51.   Free or bargain-priced items offered to encourage customers to buy a product

_____ 52.   Advertising that appears on various items such as coffee mugs, pens, and calendars, designed to help keep a company's name in front of customers

_____ 53.   Brief statement or video program released to the press announcing new products, management changes, sales performance, and other potential news items

_____ 54.   Discount offered by producers to wholesalers and retailers

_____ 55.   Nonsales communication that businesses have with their various audiences (includes both communication with the general public and press relations)

_____ 56.   Sales-promotion efforts aimed at inducing distributors or retailers to push a producer's products

_____ 57.   Gathering of media representatives at which companies announce new information; also called a press conference or press briefing

_____ 58.   Electronic media that invite participation by the general public

_____ 59.   Informal communication between customers and potential customers

Learning Objectives—Short Answer or Essay Questions

1. Explain what marketing intermediaries do and list their seven primary functions.

2. Explain how wholesalers and retailers function as intermediaries.

3. Discuss the key factors that influence channel design and selection.

4. Differentiate intensive, selective, and exclusive distribution strategies.

5. Identify the seven categories of customer communication.

6. Discuss the importance of integrated marketing communications.

7. Explain the purpose of defining a core marketing message.

8. Describe the use of social media in marketing communications.

Critical Thinking Questions

1. Discuss the seven key functions of wholesalers and retailers.

2.   List and briefly explain the types of store-based retailing.

3.   Define advertising, discuss different classifications of advertising, and consider its pros and cons.

Exploring the Internet

Log onto Facebook (www.facebook.com) or MySpace (www.myspace.com) and discuss how advertisers are adapting their communication efforts to this new media landscape.

True-False – Answers

1. True	6. True	11. True
2. False	7. False	12. False
3. False	8. True	13. True
4. False	9. True	14. True
5. True	10. False	15. True

Multiple Choice – Answers

1. A	7. B	13. A
2. D	8. D	14. D
3. B	9. B	15. D
4. D	10. C	16. C
5. A	11. A	17. B
6. C	12. B	

Match the Terms and Concepts with Their Definitions – Answers

1. FFF	32. MM
2. L	33. D
3. N	34. R
4. V	35. EE
5. EEE	36. A
6. RR	37. X
7. Y	38. JJ
8. DDD	39. Q
9. TT	40. UU
10. YY	41. CC
11. B	42. NN
12. G	43. H
13. J	44. DD
14. O	45. ZZ
15. QQ	46. SS
16. Z	47. E
17. U	48. F
18. M	49. OO
19. S	50. HH
20. VV	51. II
21. P	52. XX
22. C	53. BB
23. GG	54. AAA
24. T	55. LL
25. CCC	56. BBB
26. K	57. AA
27. W	58. WW
28. KK	59. GGG
29. FF	
30. PP	
31. I	

Learning Objectives – Short Answer or Essay Question – Answers

1. **Explain what marketing intermediaries do, and list their seven primary functions.**
   Marketing intermediaries, or middlemen, bring producers' products to market and help ensure that the goods and services are available in the right time, place, and amount. More specifically, intermediaries match buyers and sellers; provide market information; provide promotional and sales support; sort, standardize, and divide merchandise; transport and store the product; assume risks; and provide financing.

2. **Explain how wholesalers and retailers function as intermediaries.**
   Wholesalers buy from producers and sell to retailers, to other wholesalers, and to organizational customers such as businesses, government agencies, and institutions. Retailers buy from producers or wholesalers and sell the products to the final consumers.

3. **Discuss the key factors that influence channel design and selection.**
   Channel design and selection are influenced by the type of product and industry practices. They are also influenced by a firm's desired market coverage (intense, selective, or exclusive), financial ability, desire for control, and potential for channel conflict.

4. **Differentiate intensive, selective, and exclusive distribution strategies.**
   With an intensive distribution strategy, a company attempts to saturate the market with its products by offering them in every available outlet. Companies that use a more selective approach to distribution choose a limited number of retailers that can adequately support the product. Firms that use exclusive distribution grant a single wholesaler or retailer the exclusive right to sell the product within a given geographic area.

5. **Identify the seven categories of customer communication.**
   The seven basic categories of promotion are (1) personal selling, which involves contacting customers by phone, interactive media, or in person to make a sale; (2) advertising, which is a paid sponsored message transmitted by mass communication media; (3) direct marketing, which is the distribution of promotional material to customers via direct mail, e-mail, telemarketing, or the Internet to generate an order or other customer response; (4) sales promotion, which includes a number of tools designed to stimulate customer interest in a product and encourage a purchase; (5) public relations, which includes nonsales communications between businesses and their stakeholders to foster positive relationships; (6) social media, which involves efforts to influence and support the interaction of customers and product enthusiasts; and (7) post-sales communication, which helps ensure high levels of customer satisfaction and repeat business.

6. **Discuss the use of integrated marketing communications.**
   When companies use a greater variety of marketing communications, the likelihood of sending conflicting marketing messages to consumers increases. Integrated marketing communications (IMC) is a process of coordinating all of a company's communications and promotional efforts so that they present only one consistent message to the marketplace. Properly implemented, IMC increases marketing and promotional effectiveness.

7. **Explain the purpose of defining a core marketing message.**

   The core marketing message is the single most important idea you hope to convey to the target audience about your product or your company. Ideally, the message can be expressed in a single sentence. All communication effort can then expand on the core message as appropriate.

8. **Describe the use of social media in marketing communications.**

   With social media, the vital concepts are *enabling*, *influencing*, and *responding*—not *controlling*. Unlike advertising and direct mail, with social media marketers cannot control what is being said about their companies and their products. Instead, marketers should focus on *enabling* online conversations among customers and product enthusiasts; *influencing* the conversation by offering useful, interesting, and entertaining information; and *responding* whenever people have questions or criticisms.

Critical Thinking Questions - Answers

1. **Discuss the seven key functions of wholesalers and retailers.**

   Wholesalers and retailers are instrumental in creating place, time, and possession utility. They provide an efficient process for transferring products from the producer to the customer, they reduce the number of transactions, and they ensure that goods and services are available at a convenient time and place for customers. To accomplish these goals, wholesalers and retailers perform a number of specific distribution functions that make life easier for both producers and customers:

   - <u>Match buyers and sellers</u>. By making sellers' products available to multiple buyers, intermediaries reduce the number of transactions between producers and customers.
   - <u>Provide market information</u>. Intermediaries collect valuable data about customer purchases: who buys, how often, and how much. Collecting such data allows them to spot buying patterns and to share marketplace information with producers.
   - <u>Provide promotional and sales support</u>. Many intermediaries assist with marketing activities, such as creating in-store displays or advising shoppers on product choices.
   - <u>Gather assortments of goods</u>. Intermediaries receive bulk shipments from producers and break them into more convenient units by sorting, standardizing, and dividing bulk quantities into smaller packages.
   - <u>Transport and store products</u>. Intermediaries frequently maintain an inventory of merchandise that they acquire from producers so they can quickly fill customers' orders.
   - <u>Assume risks</u>. When intermediaries accept goods from manufacturers, they often take on the risks associated with damage, theft, product perishability, and obsolescence.
   - <u>Provide financing</u>. Large intermediaries sometimes provide loans to smaller producers.

2. List and briefly explain the types of store-based retailing.

Store-based retailing includes everything from newsstands to malls, but the most significant forms to study from a marketing perspective are *specialty stores*, *department stores*, *category killers*, and *discount stores*.

When you shop in a pet store, a shoe store, or a stationery store, for instance, you are in a specialty store—a store that carries only particular types of goods. The basic merchandising strategy of a specialty shop is to offer a limited number of product lines but an extensive selection of brands, styles, sizes, models, colors, materials, and prices within each line. The range and variety of specialty stores is practically endless, from florists and bridal shops to antique dealers and party-supply stores.

Category killers are supersized specialty stores that dominate a particular product category by stocking every conceivable variety of merchandise in every important product line in that category—often at prices that smaller specialty stores can't match. The Home Depot (tools and home improvement), Staples (office supplies), and Bed, Bath and Beyond (home products) are well-known category killers.

Department stores are the classic major retailers in the United States, with the likes of Bloomingdale's, Macy's, Nordstrom, Dillard's, Kohl's, Sears, and J.C. Penney. These stores can have local, regional, or national presence and different price and quality offerings, but most tend to carry clothing, housewares, bedding, furniture in some cases, and similar items. Shopping malls often feature them as *anchors*, stores with wide appeal that mall developers can count on to bring in business for all the shops in the mall.

Wal-Mart and Target are good examples of discount stores, stores that tend to be fairly large, with a wide variety of aggressively priced merchandise. Some offer few services, whereas others offer a range of services from film processing to banking. Larger discount stores such as Wal-Mart are often called *mass merchandisers*. The largest are sometimes called *supercenters*, which combine discount stores with grocery stores.

3. Define advertising, discuss different classifications of advertising, and consider its pros and cons.

Advertising consists of messages paid for by an identified sponsor and transmitted through mass communication media, or channels, including television, radio, newspapers, magazines, or online media (other than a company's own website). The two most basic categories of advertising are product advertising, which promotes specific goods and services, and institutional advertising, which is intended to create goodwill among stakeholders and build a desired image for a company or other organization. Advertising can also be classified according to the sponsor. National advertising is sponsored by companies that sell products on a nationwide basis. The term *national* refers to the level of the advertiser, not the geographic coverage of the ad. Local advertising is sponsored by a local merchant. Cooperative advertising is a cross between national and local; in these arrangements, companies with products sold nationally share the costs of local advertising with local wholesalers or retailers.

Depending on the medium, advertising can be a cost-effective way to reach thousands or even millions of potential buyers at once. However, to be effective, your messages must be persuasive, must stand out from the competition's messages, and must motivate your target audience to respond—a lofty goal considering that the average "plugged-in" U.S. resident (someone with regular mobile phone and web usage habits) sees an estimated 3,000 to 5,000 promotional messages every day.

Exploring the Internet

Log onto Facebook (www.facebook.com) or MySpace (www.myspace.com) and discuss how advertisers are adapting their communication efforts to this new media landscape.

Today's smart companies are learning to adapt their communication efforts to this new media landscape and to welcome customers' participation. With social media, the vital concepts are enabling, influencing, and responding—not controlling. Unlike advertising and direct mail, with social media marketers cannot control what is being said about their companies and their products. And unethical attempts at doing so, such as writing fake blogs, or *flogs*, in which a company insider masquerades as an adoring customer, for example, quickly bring the wrath of the online community as soon as they are unmasked.

You should be noting how marketers focus on *enabling* online conversations among customers and product enthusiasts (such as by supporting social commerce efforts that let customers submit product reviews); *influencing* the conversation by offering useful, interesting, and entertaining information; and *responding* whenever people have questions or criticisms.

Chapter 12
Management Functions and Skills

Learning Objectives
After reading this chapter, you should be able to:

1. Define the four basic management functions.
2. Outline the strategic planning process.
3. Explain the purpose of a mission statement.
4. Discuss the benefits of SWOT analysis.
5. Explain the importance of setting long-term goals and objectives.
6. Cite three common leadership styles and explain why no one style is best.
7. Identify and explain four important types of managerial skills.
8. Summarize the six steps involved in the decision-making process.

True-False
Indicate whether the statement is generally true or false by placing a "T" or an "F" in the space provided. If it is a false statement, correct it so that it becomes a true statement.

_____ 1. One role of a manager is to distribute information to employees, other managers, and other stakeholders.

_____ 2. Planning can be considered the primary management function because it drives all the other functions.

_____ 3. Strategic plans outline the firm's short-term organizational goals and set a course of action the firm will pursue to reach its goals.

_____ 4. A company's vision should be a realistic and achievable view of the future that grows out of and improves on the present.

_____ 5. SWOT stands for strategic weaknesses and organizational threats.

_____ 6. Weaknesses are negative internal factors that inhibit the company's success, such as obsolete facilities, inadequate financial resources to fund the company's growth, or lack of managerial depth and talent.

_____ 7. A goal is a broad, long-range accomplishment that the organization wants to attain in typically five or more years.

_____ 8. The goal of crisis management is to keep the company functioning smoothly both during and after a crisis.

_____ 9. Removing layers of middle management from the organizational structure is known as flattening.

_____ 10. Leadership is the rational, intellectual, and practical side of guiding an organization, and management is the inspirational, visionary, and emotional side.

_____ 11. Self-regulated managers have the ability to control or reduce disruptive impulses and moods.

_____ 12. Transformational leaders tend to focus on meeting established goals, making sure employees understand their roles in the organization, and making sure the correct resources are in place.

_____ 13. The set of underlying values, norms, and practices shared by members of an organization is known as corporate or organizational culture.

_____ 14. Quality is a measure of how closely goods or services conform to predetermined standards and customer expectations.

_____ 15. Decision-making skills involve the ability to define problems and select the best course of action.

Multiple Choice
Circle the best answer for each of the following questions.

1. Which of the following are the four basic functions of management?
   a. Planning, organizing, leading, and controlling
   b. Leadership, integrity, communication, and delegation
   c. Informational, interpersonal, decisional and planning
   d. None of the above

2. Which of the following would be considered an interpersonal role of a manager?
   a. Providing leadership to employees
   b. Acting as a liaison between groups and individuals both inside and outside the company
   c. Deciding how to respond to a customer complaint
   d. Both a and b

3. A good strategic plan answers which of the following questions?
   a. Where are we going?
   b. How do we get there?
   c. What is the business environment going to be like?
   d. All of the above

4. Which of the following are not steps in the strategic planning process?
   a. Developing a clear vision and creating a mission statement
   b. Performing a SWOT analysis, and developing forecasts
   c. Scheduling day-to-day operational tasks
   d. Analyzing the competition and developing action plans

5. A company's mission statement should include all of the following except:
   a. A brief articulation of why your organization exists
   b. A description of the company's management team
   c. What it seeks to accomplish
   d. The principles that the company will adhere to as it tries to reach its goals

6. When performing a SWOT analysis, which of the following would be considered internal factors?
   a. Strengths and opportunities
   b. Strengths and weaknesses
   c. Weaknesses and threats
   d. Opportunities and threats

7. Of the following statements, which best describes the differentiation strategy?
   a. Concentrating on a specific segment of the market, seeking to develop a better understanding of those customers and to tailor products specifically to their needs
   b. Producing or selling products more efficiently and economically than competitors
   c. Developing a level of service, a product image, unique product features (including quality), or new technologies that distinguish its product from competitors' products
   d. None of the above

8. Which of the following best describes an operational plan?
   a. Defining actions for less than one year and focusing on accomplishing specific objectives
   b. Laying out the actions and the allocation of resources necessary to achieve specific, short-term objectives
   c. Outlining the firm's long-range organizational goals and setting a course of action the firm will pursue to reach its goals
   d. All of the above

9. Positions at this level include supervisor, department head, and office manager:
   a. Top managers
   b. First-line managers
   c. Middle managers
   d. None of the above

10. Which of the following terms refers to a manager's ability to recognize his/her own feelings and the effect those feelings have on his/her own job performance and on the people around him/her?
    a. Social skills
    b. Empathy
    c. Self-awareness
    d. Motivation

11. Laissez-faire leaders:
    a. Delegate authority and involve employees in decision making
    b. Give employees the power to make decisions that apply to their specific aspects of work
    c. Control the decision-making process in their organizations
    d. None of the above

12. Change presents a major leadership challenge because:
    a. Most people don't like it
    b. They fear the unknown
    c. They may be unwilling to give up current habits or benefits
    d. All of the above

13. The manager's role of controlling includes all of the following except:
    a. Managing the finance and accounting functions of an organization
    b. Monitoring a firm's progress toward meeting its organizational goals and objectives
    c. Resetting the course if goals or objectives change in response to shifting conditions
    d. Correcting deviations if goals or objectives are not being attained

14. Administrative skills refer to a manager:
    a. Having the ability to communicate with other people, work effectively with them, motivate them, and lead
    b. Possessing the knowledge and ability to perform the mechanics of a particular job
    c. Having the ability to make schedules, gather information, analyze data, plan, and organize
    d. Possessing the ability to see organizations, systems, and markets both as complete entities in the context of their environments and as interrelated

pieces of a whole

Match the Terms and Concepts with Their Definitions

A. administrative skills	S. management pyramid
B. autocratic leaders	T. managerial roles
C. balanced scorecard	U. mentoring
D. benchmarking	V. middle managers
E. coaching	W. mission statement
F. conceptual skills	X. objective
G. controlling	Y. operational plans
H. corporate culture	Z. organizing
I. crisis management	AA. participative management
J. decision-making skills	BB. planning
K. democratic leaders	CC. quality
L. empowerment	DD. standards
M. first-line managers	EE. strategic plans
N. goal	FF. tactical plans
O. interpersonal skills	GG. technical skills
P. laissez-faire leaders	HH. top managers
Q. leading	II. vision
R. management	

_____ 1.   Process of coordinating resources to meet organizational goals

_____ 2.   Behavioral patterns and activities involved in carrying out the functions of management; includes interpersonal, informational, and decisional roles

_____ 3.   Establishing objectives and goals for an organization and determining the best ways to accomplish them

_____ 4.   Plans that establish the actions and the resource allocation required to accomplish strategic goals; they are usually defined for periods of two to five years and developed by top managers

_____ 5.   A viable view of the future that is rooted in but improves on the present

_____ 6.   A statement of the organization's purpose, basic goals, and philosophies

_____ 7.   Broad, long-range target or aim

_____ 8.   Specific, short-range target or aim

_____ 9.   Plans that define the actions and the resource allocation necessary to achieve tactical objectives and to support strategic plans

_____ 10.   Plans that lay out the actions and the resource allocation needed to achieve operational objectives and to support tactical plans

_____ 11.   Procedures and systems for minimizing the harm that might result from some unusually threatening situations

_____ 12.   Process of arranging resources to carry out the organization's plans

_____ 13.   Organizational structure comprising top, middle, and lower management

_____ 14.   Those at the highest level of the organization's management hierarchy; they are responsible for setting strategic goals, and they have the most power and responsibility in the organization

_____ 15.   Those in the middle of the management hierarchy; they develop plans to implement the goals of top managers and coordinate the work of first-line managers

_____ 16.   Those at the lowest level of the management hierarchy; they supervise the operating employees and implement the plans set at the higher management levels; also called supervisory managers

_____ 17.   Process of guiding and motivating people to work toward organizational goals

_____ 18.   Leaders who do not involve others in decision making

_____ 19.   Leaders who delegate authority and involve employees in decision making

_____ 20.   Philosophy of allowing employees to take part in planning and decision making

_____ 21.   Leaders who leave the most instances of decision making up to employees, particularly concerning day-to-day matters

_____ 22.   Granting decision-making and problem-solving authorities to employees so they can act without getting approval from management

_____ 23.   Helping employees reach their highest potential by meeting with them, discussing problems that hinder their ability to work effectively, and offering suggestions and encouragement to overcome these problems

_____ 24.   Experienced managers guiding less-experienced colleagues in nuances of office politics, serving as role models for appropriate business behavior, and helping to negotiate the corporate structure

_____ 25.   A set of shared values and norms that support the management system and guide management and employee behavior

_____ 26.   Process of measuring progress against goals and objectives and correcting deviations if results are not as expected

_____ 27.   Method of monitoring the performance from four perspectives: finances, operations, customer relationships, and the growth and development of employees and intellectual property

_____ 28.   A measure of how closely a product conforms to predetermined standards and customer expectations

_____ 29.   Criteria against which performance is measured

_____ 30.   Collecting and comparing process and performance data from other companies

_____ 31.   Skills required to understand other people and to interact effectively with them

_____ 32.   Ability and knowledge to perform the mechanics of a particular job

_____ 33.   Technical skills in information gathering, data analysis, planning, organizing, and other aspects of managerial work

_____ 34.   Ability to understand the relationship of parts to the whole

_____ 35.   Ability to identify a decision situation, analyze the problem, weigh the alternatives, choose an alternative, implement it, and evaluate the results

Learning Objectives—Short Answer or Essay Questions

1. Define the four basic management functions.

2. Outline the strategic planning process.

3. Explain the purpose of a mission statement.

4. Discuss the benefits of SWOT analysis.

5. Explain the importance of setting long-term goals and objectives.

6. Cite three common leadership styles and explain why no one style is best.

7. Identify and explain four important types of managerial skills.

8. Summarize the six steps involved in the decision-making process.

Critical Thinking Questions

1. Discuss why managers need to forecast and briefly describe the two major categories of forecasting.

2.   List a set of questions that you can use as a tool to determine someone's readiness for leadership; briefly discuss the significance of each.

3.   List and explain the four steps in the organizational change process.

True-False – Answers

1. True	6. False	11. True
2. True	7. True	12. False
3. False	8. True	13. True
4. True	9. True	14. True
5. False	10. False	15. True

Multiple Choice – Answers

1. A	10. C
2. D	11. B
3. D	12. D
4. C	13. A
5. B	14. C
6. B	
7. C	
8. A	
9. B	

Match the Terms and Concepts with Their Definitions – Answers

1. R	12. Z	24. U
2. T	13. S	25. H
3. BB	14. HH	26. G
4. EE	15. V	27. C
5. II	16. M	28. CC
6. W	17. Q	29. DD
7. N	18. B	30. D
8. X	19. K	31. O
9. FF	20. AA	32. GG
10. Y	21. P	33. A
11. I	22. L	34. F
	23. E	35. J

Learning Objectives – Short Answer or Essay Question – Answers

1. **Define the four basic management functions.**
   The four management functions are (1) planning—establishing objectives and goals for the organization and translating them into action plans; (2) organizing—arranging resources to carry out the organization's plans; (3) leading—influencing and motivating people to work effectively and willingly toward company goals; and (4) controlling—monitoring progress toward organizational goals, resetting the course if goals or objectives change in response to shifting conditions, and correcting deviations if goals or objectives are not being attained.

2. **Outline the strategic planning process.**
   The strategic planning process begins with a clear vision for the company's future. This vision is then translated into a mission statement so it can be shared with all members of the organization. Next, managers assess the company's strengths, weaknesses, opportunities, and threats; they develop forecasts about future trends that affect their industry and products; and they analyze the competition—paying close attention to their strengths and weaknesses so that they can use this information to gain a competitive edge. Managers use this information to establish company goals and objectives. Finally, they translate these goals and objectives into action plans.

3. **Explain the purpose of a mission statement.**
   A mission statement defines why the organization exists, what it does, what it hopes to achieve, and the principles it will abide by to meet its goals. It is used to bring clarity of focus to members of the organization and to provide guidelines for the adoption of future projects.

4. **Discuss the benefits of SWOT analysis.**
An organization identifies its strengths, weaknesses, opportunities, and threats prior to establishing long-term goals. Identifying internal strengths and weaknesses gives the firm insight into its current abilities. The organization must then decide whether new abilities must be learned to meet current or more ambitious goals. Internal strengths become a firm's core competence if they are a bundle of skills and technologies that set the company apart from competitors. Identifying a firm's external opportunities and threats helps prepare it for challenges that might interfere with its ability to reach its goals.

5. **Explain the importance of setting long-term goals and objectives.**
Goals and objectives establish long- and short-range targets that help managers fulfill the company's mission. Setting appropriate goals increases employee motivation, establishes standards by which individual and group performance can be measured, guides employee activity, and clarifies management's expectations.

6. **Cite three common leadership styles, and explain why no one style is best.**
Three common leadership styles are autocratic, democratic, and laissez-faire (also called free-rein). Each may work best in a given situation: autocratic when quick decisions are needed, democratic when employee participation in decision making is desirable, and laissez-faire when fostering creativity is a priority. Good leaders are flexible enough to respond with the best approach for the situation.

7. **Identify and explain four important types of managerial skills.**
Managers use interpersonal skills to communicate with other people, work effectively with them, and lead them; technical skills to perform the mechanics of a particular job; administrative skills to manage an organization efficiently; conceptual skills to see the organization as a whole, to see it in the context of its environment, and to understand how the various parts interrelate; and decision-making skills to ensure that the best decisions are made.

8. **Summarize the six steps involved in the decision-making process.**
The decision-making process begins by recognizing that a problem or opportunity exists. Next, managers identify and develop options using a variety of brainstorming techniques. Once the options have been put forth, they analyze the options using appropriate criteria. Then they select the best option, implement the decision, and monitor the results, making changes as needed.

Critical Thinking Questions - Answers

1. **Discuss why managers need to forecast and briefly describe the two major categories of forecasting.**

   By its very nature, planning requires managers to predict the future, even if it's only making the assumption that all the employees currently working a project will still be working on it next week or next month. Forecasting is a notoriously difficult and error-prone part of strategic planning. Not only do you need to predict what will (or will not) occur, but when it will occur and how it will affect your business. Moreover, the range of variables that must be predicted is immense—everything from product demand to the appearance of new competitors to changes in government regulations. At the same time, forecasting is crucial to every company's success because it influences the decisions managers make regarding virtually every business activity.

   Managerial forecasts fall under two broad categories: quantitative forecasts, which are typically based on historical data or tests and often involve complex statistical computations, and qualitative forecasts, which are based more on intuitive judgments. Statistically analyzing the cycles of economic growth and recession over several decades to predict when the economy will take a downward turn is an example of quantitative forecasting. Making predictions about sales of a new product on the basis of experience or the likely response of competitors to the new product are examples of qualitative forecasting. Neither method is foolproof, but both are valuable tools, helping managers to fill in the unknown variables that inevitably crop up in the planning process.

   Regardless of the type of forecast or the variables being predicted, reliable inputs are key. Forecasters collect pertinent data and information in a wide variety of ways, such as reviewing internal data, conducting surveys and other research, purchasing industry forecasts from research companies that specialize in particular industries, and reviewing projections from the many periodicals, industry organizations, and government agencies that publish forecasts on business and economic issues.

2. **List a set of questions that you can use as a tool to determine someone's readiness for leadership; briefly discuss the significance of each.**

   - <u>Can they listen?</u> Can they truly listen to what people mean to say, not just what they actually say or what they want to hear?
   - <u>Can they communicate?</u> If they find themselves frequently being misunderstood, for whatever reason, consider this a warning that they need to improve their communication skills.
   - <u>Can they lead by example?</u> Are they a living, breathing example of what they want the organization to be?
   - <u>Are they dedicated to the organization's success above their own?</u> Leaders who put personal power or wealth ahead of the organization's success may shine brightly, but they usually shine briefly.

- <u>Do they know what makes other people tick?</u> Knowing what motivates the diverse people around they is crucial to leading them all in the same direction.
- <u>Do they manage themselves well?</u> If they can't get their own work done, whether it's meeting deadlines or developing the skills they lack, their shortcomings will be amplified throughout the organization. For instance, if they're constantly late when making major decisions, they'll slow down every employee affected by those decisions.
- <u>Are they willing to accept responsibility?</u> Business leaders sometimes need to make tough decisions that affect the lives of hundreds or thousands of people; will they be ready when it's time to make the tough call or to accept blame for company mistakes?
- <u>Can they face reality?</u> Whether they're blinded by their own egos or just simple optimism, leaders who refuse to see the world the way it really exists usually set their companies up for failure.
- <u>Can they solve problems but stay focused on opportunities?</u> Leaders who get mired in problems miss opportunities; those who look only at opportunities can get bitten by problems that they should have solved.
- <u>Are they willing to trust their employees?</u> If they cannot delegate responsibility, they will swamp themselves with too much work and hinder the growth of their employees.

3. **List and explain the four steps in the organizational change process.**

- <u>Identify what needs to change.</u> Changes can involve the structure of the organization, technologies and systems, or people's attitudes, beliefs, skills, or behaviors.
- <u>Identify the forces acting for and against the change.</u> By understanding these forces, managers can work to amplify the forces that will facilitate the change and remove or diminish the negative forces. For instance, if uncertainty is one of the forces working against the change, education and communication may help reduce these forces and thereby reduce resistance to the change.
- <u>Choose the approach, or combination of approaches, best suited to the situation.</u> Managers can institute change through a variety of techniques, including communication, education, participation in the decision making, negotiation with groups opposed to the change, visible support from top managers or other opinion leaders, or coercive use of authority (usually recommended only for crisis situations). Helping people understand the need for change is often called unfreezing existing behaviors.
- <u>Reinforce changed behavior and monitor continued progress.</u> Once the change has been made, managers need to reinforce new behaviors and make sure old behaviors don't creep back in. This effort is commonly called refreezing new behaviors.

Chapter 13
Organization, Teamwork, and Motivation

Learning Objectives
After reading this chapter, you should be able to:

1. Discuss the function of a company's organization structure.
2. Explain the concepts of accountability, authority, and delegation.
3. Define five major types of organization structure.
4. Highlight the advantages and disadvantages of working in teams.
5. List the characteristics of effective teams.
6. Review the five stages of team development and highlight six causes of team conflict.
7. Compare Maslow's hierarchy of needs and Herzberg's two-factor theory, then explain their application to employee motivation.
8. Explain why expectancy theory is considered by some to be the best description of employee behavior.

True-False
Indicate whether the statement is generally true or false by placing a "T" or an "F" in the space provided. If it is a false statement, correct it so that it becomes a true statement.

_____ 1.   A poorly designed organizational structure can create enormous waste, confusion, and frustration for a company's employees, suppliers, and customers.

_____ 2.   A company's formal organization is the network of interactions that develop on a personal level among workers.

_____ 3.   Overemphasis on job specialization can lead employees to focus so intently on their own responsibilities that it may reduce their contribution to the organization's overall success.

_____ 4.   A line organization has a clear line of authority flowing from the top down.

_____ 5.   The number of people a manager directly supervises is called span of control.

_____ 6.   A divisional structure attempts to overcome drawbacks of other structures by pooling and sharing a company's resources across divisions and functional groups.

_____ 7.   Teams differ from work groups in that teams interact primarily to share information and to make decisions to help one another perform within each member's area of responsibility.

_____ 8.   Groupthink occurs when peer pressure causes individual team members to withhold contrary or unpopular opinions.

_____ 9.   Conflict within a team can be good.

_____ 10.   Need is the combination of forces that moves individuals to take certain actions and avoid others in pursuit of individual objectives.

_____ 11.   Esteem needs refers to the need to become everything one can become.

_____ 12.   Hygiene factors are associated with satisfying experiences.

_____ 13.   Extrinsic rewards are those given by other people, such as money, promotions, and tenure.

_____ 14.   Equity theory links an employee's efforts with the outcome he or she expects from that effort.

_____ 15.   Negative reinforcement refers to punishment for not behaving in the desired way.

Multiple Choice

Circle the best answer for each of the following questions.

1. A well-designed structure helps the company achieve its goals by:
    a. Providing a framework for managers to divide responsibilities
    b. Effectively distributing the authority to make decisions
    c. Coordinating and controlling the organization's work
    d. All of the above

2. Division of labor is:
    a. The degree to which organizational tasks are broken down into separate jobs
    b. The amount of control a particular manager has over an employee
    c. Another term for "job sharing"
    d. All of the above

3. The obligation for a person to perform certain duties and achieve the goals and objectives associated with that job is known as:
    a. Accountability
    b. Authority
    c. Responsibility
    d. Delegation

4. An organization with relatively few levels in the management hierarchy is referred to as:
    a. A tall organization
    b. A flat organization
    c. A matrix organization
    d. None of the above

5. Organizations that focus decision-making authority near the top of the chain of command are said to be:
    a. Centralized
    b. Decentralized
    c. Bureaucratic
    d. None of the above

6. The vertical structure of an organization refers to:
    a. The number of business functions and work specialties across a company
    b. The number of layers the chain of command is divided into from the top of a company to the bottom
    c. The arrangement of activities into logical groups that are then clustered into larger departments
    d. None of the above

7. Which of the following is not a benefit of splitting an organization into separate functional departments?
    a. It allows for the efficient use of resources and encourages the development of in-depth skills
    b. It centralizes decision making and enables unified direction by top management
    c. It enhances communication and the coordination of activities within departments
    d. It simplifies communication, coordination, and control when it becomes more complicated and geographically dispersed

8. Cross-functional teams:
    a. Draw together employees from various functional areas and expertise
    b. Are organized along the lines of the organization's vertical structure
    c. Are assembled to find ways of improving quality, efficiency, or other performance issues
    d. Are groups of physically dispersed members who communicate electronically

9. In the storming phase of team development, team members:
    a. Show more of their personalities and become more assertive in establishing their roles
    b. Determine what types of behaviors are appropriate within the group, and identify what is expected of them
    c. Come to understand and accept one another, reach a consensus on who the leader is, and reach agreement on what each member's roles are
    d. Are really committed to the team's goals, solve problems, and handle disagreements with maturity in the interest of task accomplishment

10. Team conflicts can arise for which of the following reasons:
    a. Individual team members feel they are in competition for resources
    b. Team members may disagree about who is responsible for a specific task
    c. Poorly defined responsibilities and job boundaries
    d. All of the above

11. A productive agenda answers all of the following questions except:
    a. What do we need to do in this meeting to accomplish our goals?
    b. What will the resulting action items be?
    c. What issues will be of greatest importance to all participants?
    d. What information must be available in order to discuss these issues?

12. All of the following people are considered pioneers in the study of workplace motivation except:
    a. Fredrick W. Taylor
    b. Abraham Maslow
    c. W. Michael Donovan
    d. Fredrick Herzberg

13. The need to give and receive love and to feel a sense of belonging is this category of Maslow's hierarchy:
    a. Social
    b. Safety
    c. Self-esteem
    d. Physiological

14. Managers who believe that employees dislike work and can be motivated only by the fear of losing their jobs or by extrinsic rewards are said to have this orientation:
    a. Theory X
    b. Theory Y
    c. Theory Z
    d. None of the above

15. Which of the following refers to a collaborative goal-setting process where managers and employees define the goals, responsibilities, and the means of evaluating individual or group performance:
    a. Management by exception
    b. Management by objective
    c. Management by walking around
    d. None of the above

Match the Terms and Concepts with Their Definitions

A.	accountability	Z.	line-and-staff organization
B.	authority	AA.	management by objectives
C.	behavior modification	BB.	matrix structure
D.	centralization	CC.	morale
E.	chain of command	DD.	motivation
F.	cohesiveness	EE.	motivators
G.	committee	FF.	network structure
H.	cross-functional teams	GG.	norms
I.	decentralization	HH.	organization chart
J.	delegation	II.	organization structure
K.	departmentalization	JJ.	problem-solving team
L.	divisional structure	KK.	reinforcement theory
M.	engagement	LL.	responsibility
N.	equity theory	MM.	scientific management
O.	expectancy theory	NN.	self-managed teams
P.	flat organizations	OO.	span of management
Q.	formal organization	PP.	tall organizations
R.	free riders	QQ.	task force
S.	functional structure	RR.	team
T.	functional teams	SS.	Theory X
U.	goal-setting theory	TT.	Theory Y
V.	hybrid structure	UU.	Theory Z
W.	hygiene factors	VV.	virtual teams
X.	informal organization	WW.	work specialization
Y.	line organization		

_____ 1.   Power granted by the organization to make decisions, take actions, and allocate resources

_____ 2.   Framework that enables managers to divide responsibilities, ensure employee accountability, and distribute decision-making authority

_____ 3.   Managerial assumption that employees are irresponsible, are unambitious, and dislike work, and that managers must use force, control, or threats to motivate them

_____ 4.   Diagram showing how employees and tasks are grouped and where the lines of communication and authority flow

_____ 5.   A framework officially established by managers for accomplishing the organization's tasks

_____ 6.   Networks of informal employee interactions that are not defined by the formal structure

_____ 7.   Specialization in or responsibility for some portion of an organization's overall work tasks; also called division of labor

_____ 8.   Pathway for the flow of authority from one management level to the next

_____ 9.   Obligation to perform the duties and achieve the goals and objectives associated with a position

_____ 10.   Obligation to report results and to justify outcomes that fall below expectations

_____ 11.   Assignment of work and the authority and responsibility required to complete it

_____ 12.   Chain-of-command system that establishes a clear line of authority flowing from the top down

_____ 13.   The combination of forces that moves individuals to take certain actions and behaviors and avoid other actions or behaviors

_____ 14.   Number of people under one manager's control; also known as span of control

_____ 15.   Organizations with a wide span of management and few hierarchical levels

_____ 16.   Organizations with a narrow span of management and many hierarchical levels

_____ 17. Concentration of decision-making authority at the top of the organization

_____ 18. Delegation of decision-making authority to employees in lower-level positions

_____ 19. Grouping people within an organization according to function, division, matrix, or network

_____ 20. Grouping workers according to their similar skills, resource use, and expertise

_____ 21. Grouping departments according to similarities in product, process, customer, or geography

_____ 22. Structure that uses functional and divisional patterns simultaneously

_____ 23. Virtual organization in which a company relies on multiple external partners to complete its business model

_____ 24. Structure that combines elements of functional, divisional, matrix, and network organizations

_____ 25. A unit of two or more people who share a mission and collective responsibility as they work together to achieve a common goal

_____ 26. Informal team that meets to find ways of improving quality, efficiency, and the work environment

_____ 27. Teams in which members are responsible for an entire process or operation

_____ 28. Teams whose members come from a single functional department and that are based on the organization's vertical structure

_____ 29. Teams that draw together employees from different functional areas

_____ 30. Team of people from several departments who are temporarily brought together to address a specific issue

_____ 31. Team that may become a permanent part of the organization and is designed to deal with regularly recurring tasks

_____ 32. Teams that use communication technology to bring geographically distant employees together to achieve goals

_____ 33. Team members who do not contribute sufficiently to the group's activities because members are not being held individually accountable for their work

_____ 34. A measure of how committed the team members are to their team's goals

_____ 35. Informal standards of conduct that guide team behavior

_____ 36. An employee's rational and emotional commitment to his or her work

_____ 37. Attitude an individual has toward his or her job and employer

_____ 38. Line organization that adds functional groups of people who provide advice and specialized services

_____ 39. Management approach designed to improve employees' efficiency by scientifically studying their work

_____ 40. In Herzberg's two-factor model, aspects of the work environment that are associated with dissatisfaction

_____ 41. In Herzberg's two-factor model, factors that may increase motivation

_____ 42. Leadership approach that emphasizes involving employees at all levels and treating them like family

_____ 43. A theory that suggests employees base their level of satisfaction on the ratio of their inputs to the job and the outputs or rewards they receive from it

_____ 44. Suggests that the effort employees put into their work depends on expectations about their own ability to perform, expectations about likely rewards, and the attractiveness of those rewards

_____ 45. Motivational theory suggesting that setting goals can be an effective way to motivate employees

_____ 46. A motivational approach in which managers and employees work together to structure personal goals and objectives for every individual, department, and project to mesh with the organization's goals

_____ 47. A motivational approach based on the idea that managers can motivate employees by influencing their behaviors with positive and negative reinforcement

_____ 48. Systematic use of rewards and punishments to change human behavior

_____ 49. Managerial assumption that employees enjoy meaningful work, are naturally committed to certain goals, are capable of creativity, and seek out responsibility under the right conditions

Learning Objectives—Short Answer or Essay Questions

1. Discuss the function of a company's organization structure.

2. Explain the concepts of accountability, authority, and delegation.

3. Define five major types of organization structure.

4. Highlight the advantages and disadvantages of working in teams.

5. List the characteristics of effective teams.

6. Review the five stages of team development and highlight six causes of team conflict.

7. Compare Maslow's hierarchy of needs and Herzberg's two-factor theory, then explain their application to employee motivation.

8. Explain why expectancy theory is considered by some to be the best description of employee behavior.

Critical Thinking Questions

1. Discuss ways that team leaders and team members can avoid conflict within a team.

2.   Discuss equity theory and how the concept of equity impacts a business.

3.   Discuss the factors of goal setting and reinforcement relative to a manager's use of motivational strategies.

True-False – Answers

1. True	6. False	11. False
2. False	7. False	12. False
3. True	8. True	13. True
4. True	9. True	14. False
5. True	10. False	15. True

Multiple Choice – Answers

1. D	7. D	13. A
2. A	8. A	14. A
3. C	9. A	15. B
4. B	10. D	
5. A	11. B	
6. B	12. C	

Match the Terms and Concepts with Their Definitions – Answers

1. B	18. I	35. GG
2. II	19. K	36. M
3. SS	20. S	37. CC
4. HH	21. L	38. Z
5. Q	22. BB	39. MM
6. X	23. FF	40. W
7. WW	24. V	41. EE
8. E	25. RR	42. UU
9. LL	26. JJ	43. N
10. A	27. NN	44. O
11. J	28. T	45. U
12. Y	29. H	46. AA
13. DD	30. QQ	47. KK
14. OO	31. G	48. C
15. O	32. VV	49. TT
16. PP	33. R	
17. D	34. F	

Learning Objectives – Short Answer or Essay Question – Answers

1. **Discuss the function of a company's organization structure.**
   An organization's structure provides a framework through which a company can coordinate and control the work, divide responsibilities, distribute authority, and hold employees accountable. An organization chart provides a visual representation of this framework.

2. **Explain the concepts of accountability, authority, and delegation.**
   Accountability is the obligation to report work results to supervisors or team members and to justify any outcomes that fall below expectations. Authority is the power to make decisions, issue orders, carry out actions, and allocate resources to achieve the organization's goals. Delegation is the assignment of work and the transfer of authority and responsibility to complete that work.

3. **Define five major types of organization structure.**
   Companies can organize in four primary ways: by function, which groups employees according to their skills, resource use, and expertise; by division, which establishes self-contained departments formed according to similarities in product, process, customer, or geography; by matrix, which assigns employees from functional departments to interdisciplinary project teams and requires them to report to both a department head and a team leader; and by network, which connects separate companies that perform selected tasks for a headquarters organization. In addition, many companies now combine elements of two or more of these designs into hybrid structures.

4. **Highlight the advantages and disadvantages of working in teams.**

   Teamwork has the potential to produce higher-quality decisions, increase commitment to solutions and changes, lower stress and destructive internal competition, and improve flexibility and responsiveness. The potential disadvantages of working in teams include inefficiency, groupthink, diminished individual motivation, structural disruption, and excessive workloads.

5. **List the characteristics of effective teams.**

   Effective teams have a clear sense of purpose, communicate openly and honestly, build a sense of fairness in decision making, think creatively, stay focused on key issues, manage conflict constructively, and select team members wisely by involving stakeholders, creative thinkers, and members with a diversity of views. Moreover, effective teams have an optimal size of between 5 and 12 members.

6. **Review the five stages of team development, and highlight six causes of team conflict.**

   Teams typically go through five stages of development. In the forming stage, team members become acquainted with each other and with the group's purpose. In the storming stage, conflict often arises as coalitions and power struggles develop. In the norming stage, conflicts are resolved and harmony develops. In the performing stage, members focus on achieving the team's goals. In the adjourning stage, the team dissolves upon completion of its task. Team conflict can arise from competition for scarce resources; confusion over task responsibility; poor communication and misinformation; differences in values, attitudes, and personalities; power struggles; and goal incongruity.

7. **Compare Maslow's hierarchy of needs and Herzberg's two-factor theory, then explain their application to employee motivation.**

   Maslow's hierarchy organizes individual needs into five categories and proposes that the individual must satisfy the most basic needs before being able to address higher-level needs. Based on the assumption that employees want to "climb to the top" of Maslow's pyramid, managers should provide opportunities to satisfy those higher-level needs. Herzberg's two-factor theory covers the same general set of employee needs but divides them into two distinct groups. His theory suggests that hygiene factors—such as working conditions, company policies, and job security—can influence employee dissatisfaction, but an improvement in these factors will not motivate employees. Only motivational factors such as recognition and responsibility can improve employee performance.

8. **Explain why expectancy theory is considered by some to be the best description of employee behavior.**

   Expectancy, which suggests that the effort employees put into their work depends on expectations about their own ability to perform, expectations about the rewards that the organization will give in response to that performance, and the attractiveness of those rewards relative to their individual goals, is considered a good model because it considers the linkages between effort and outcome. For instance, if employees think a linkage is "broken," such as having doubts that their efforts will yield acceptable performance or worries that they will perform well but no one will notice, they're likely to put less effort into their work.

Critical Thinking Questions - Answers

1. **Discuss ways that team leaders and team members can avoid conflict within a team.**

    Teams handle conflict in a variety of ways. Depending on the strength of the team leadership and the urgency of the situation, a team may simply force a resolution to the conflict, bringing it out in the open and resolving it as quickly as possible. At the other extreme, the team leadership may choose to ignore the conflict and wait for it to subside naturally—which may only serve to quiet the arguments temporarily without actually solving the problem. Other alternatives include negotiating compromises or reminding the team to refocus on its shared goals. In the worst cases, a team may need to be disbanded or reformed with different members.

    Team members and team leaders can also take several steps to prevent conflicts. First, by establishing clear goals that engage every member, the team reduces the chance that members will battle over objectives or roles. Second, by developing well-defined tasks for each member, the team leader ensures that all parties are aware of their responsibilities and the limits of their authority. Third, by facilitating open communication, the team leader can ensure that all members understand their own tasks and objectives as well as those of their teammates. Communication builds respect and tolerance, and it provides a forum for bringing misunderstandings into the open before they turn into full-blown conflicts.

2. **Discuss equity theory and how the concept of equity impacts a business.**

    Equity theory contributes to the understanding of motivation by suggesting that employee satisfaction depends on the perceived ratio of inputs to outputs. If you work side by side with someone, doing the same job and giving the same amount of effort, only to learn that your colleague earns more money, would you be satisfied in your work and motivated to continue working hard? You perceive a state of inequity, so you probably won't be happy with the situation. In response, you might ask for a raise, decide not to work as hard, try to change perceptions of your efforts or their outcomes, or simply quit and find a new job; any one of these steps could bring your perceived input/output ratio back into balance. In the aftermath of large-scale layoffs in many sectors of the economy in the past few years, many of the employees left behind feel a sense of inequity in being asked to shoulder the work of those who left, without getting paid more for the extra effort. Equity also plays a central role in complaints about gender pay fairness and many unionizing efforts, whenever employees feel they aren't getting a fair share of corporate profits or are being asked to shoulder more than their fair share of hardships.

3. **Discuss the factors of goal setting and reinforcement relative to a manager's use of motivational strategies.**

Once managers have some idea of what raises or lowers employee motivation, they can devise policies and procedures that attempt to keep workforce energized and engaged. The range of motivational decisions managers face is almost endless, from redesigning jobs to make them more interesting to offering recognition programs for high achievers. Whether it's a basic award program for salespeople or an entirely new way to structure the workforce, though, every motivational strategy needs to consider two critical aspects: setting goals and reinforcing behavior.

Successful motivation involves action. To be successful, that action needs to be directed toward a meaningful goal. Accordingly, goal-setting theory suggests the idea that goals can motivate employees. The process of setting goals is often embodied in the technique known as management by objectives (MBO), a companywide process that empowers employees and involves them in goal setting and decision making. This process consists of four steps: setting goals, planning actions, implementing plans, and reviewing performance. Because employees at all levels are involved in all four steps, they learn more about company objectives and feel that they are an important part of the companywide team. Furthermore, they understand how even their individual job function contributes to the organization's long-term success.

One of the key elements of MBO is a collaborative goal-setting process. Together, a manager and employee define the employee's goals, the responsibilities for achieving those goals, and the means of evaluating individual and group performance so that the employee's activities are directly linked to achieving the organization's long-term goals. Jointly setting clear and challenging—but achievable—goals can encourage employees to reach higher levels of performance.

Employees in the workplace, like human beings in all aspects of life, tend to repeat behaviors that create positive outcomes. Reinforcement theory suggests that managers can motivate employees by controlling or changing their actions through behavior modification. Managers systematically encourage those actions that are desirable by providing pleasant consequences and discourage those that are not by providing unpleasant consequences.

Positive reinforcement offers pleasant consequences (such as a gift, praise, public recognition, bonus, dinner, or trip) for completing or repeating a desired action. Experts recommend the use of positive reinforcement because it emphasizes the desired behavior rather than the unwanted behavior. By contrast, negative reinforcement allows people to avoid unpleasant consequences by behaving in the desired way. For example, fear of losing a job (unpleasant consequences) may move an employee to finish a project on time (desired behavior). For motivated employees, however, negative techniques are likely to be less powerful than encouraging their sense of direction, creativity, and pride in doing a good job.

Chapter 14
Human Resources

Learning Objectives
After reading this chapter, you should be able to:

1. Explain the challenges and advantages of a diverse workforce.
2. Discuss four staffing challenges employers are facing in today's workplace.
3. Discuss four alternative work arrangements that a company can use to address workplace challenges.
4. Identify the six stages in the hiring process.
5. List six popular types of financial incentive programs for employees.
6. Highlight five popular employee benefits.
7. Describe four ways an employee's status may change and discuss why many employers like to fill job vacancies from within.
8. Define the collective bargaining process.

True-False
Indicate whether the statement is generally true or false by placing a "T" or an "F" in the space provided. If it is a false statement, correct it so that it becomes a true statement.

_____ 1. Employee burnout is a state of physical and emotional exhaustion that can result from constant exposure to stress over a long period of time.

_____ 2. Generation X refers to those born during the two decades following World War II.

_____ 3. In occupations that have traditionally been served primarily by women, such as teaching and nursing, women still earn less than men on average.

_____ 4. Working to identify potential replacements in the event of the loss of employees is known as succession planning.

_____ 5. A job description identifies the type of personnel a job requires, including the skills, education, experience, and personal attributes that candidates need to possess.

_____ 6. Effective orientation programs help employees become more productive in less time, help eliminate confusion and mistakes, and can significantly increase employee retention rates.

_____ 7. A skills inventory identifies both the current skill levels of all the employees and the skills the company needs in order to succeed.

_____ 8. In a 360-degree review a person is given feedback from subordinates, peers, and superiors.

_____ 9. Compensation refers to direct payments to employees such as wages or salary, but does not include benefits.

_____ 10. Profit sharing ties rewards to profits (or cost savings) achieved by meeting specific goals such as quality and productivity improvement.

_____ 11. Employers are under no general legal obligation to provide insurance coverage.

_____ 12. A defined benefit retirement plan is one in which companies specify how much they will put into the retirement fund (by matching employee contributions, for instance), without guaranteeing any specific payouts during retirement.

_____ 13. Outsourcing services such as résumé-writing courses, career counseling, office space, and secretarial help are offered to laid-off executives and blue-collar employees alike.

_____ 14. At-will employment means that companies are free to fire nearly anyone they choose.

_____ 15. A lockout is a court order prohibiting union workers from taking certain actions.

Multiple Choice

Circle the best answer for each of the following questions.

1. Which of the following restructures work to provide a better fit between employees' skills and their jobs?
   a. Job redesign
   b. Job enrichment
   c. Job specialization
   d. Work-life balance

2. Which of the following is a workforce diversity issue:
    a. Managing people from diverse in race, gender, age, culture, family structures, religion, sexual orientation, mental and physical ability, and educational backgrounds
    b. Managing workforce diversity to connect with customers
    c. Managing workforce diversity to take advantage of the broadest possible pool of talent
    d. All of the above

3. Those born from the early 1960s through the early 1980s are known as:
    a. Baby boomers
    b. Generation X
    c. Generation Y
    d. Millennials

4.   A scheduling system that allows employees to choose their own hours, within certain limits, is known as:
    a. Job sharing
    b. Telecommuting
    c. Flextime
    d. None of the above

5. Which of the following is not a tool for forecasting a company's demand for employees?
    a. Analyzing forecasted sales revenues
    b. Calculating the expected turnover rate
    c. Understanding how the current workforce's skill level corresponds relative to the company's future needs
    d. None of the above

6. Contingent employees are:
    a. Prospective employees
    b. Terminated employees
    c. Temporary employees
    d. None of the above

7. Employers may use pre-employment tests to assess prospective employees for which of the following?
    a. Substance abuse
    b. Integrity and personality
    c. Job skills
    d. All of the above

8. Evaluating employees relative to their ability to complete tasks specific to the position, contribution to the company's overall success, and interaction with colleagues and customers is commonly known as:
   a. Performance appraisal
   b. Employee report card
   c. Job survey
   d. None of the above

9. A payment in addition to the regular wage or salary is considered:
   a. Commission
   b. Bonus
   c. Profit sharing
   d. Pay for performance

10. Which of the following type of retirement plan is typically a defined benefit plan?
    a. 401(k) plan
    b. 403(b) plan
    c. Pension plan
    d. None of the above

11. An ESOP is:
    a. An executive stock option plan
    b. An employee stock ownership plan
    c. An employee savings program
    d. None of the above

12. Which law requires employers with 50 or more workers to provide up to 12 weeks of unpaid leave per year for childbirth, adoption, or the care of oneself, a child, a spouse, or a parent with serious illness?
    a. Sarbanes-Oxley
    b. The Civil Rights Act of 1964
    c. The Family Medical Leave Act of 1993
    d. HIPAA

13. For a national labor union, which of the following represents employees in a specific geographic area or facility:
    a. Locals
    b. Shop stewards
    c. Federations
    d. None of the above

14. When parties are required by a government agency to submit to arbitration it is known as:
    a. Binding arbitration
    b. Voluntary arbitration
    c. Compulsory arbitration
    d. Mediation

15. A temporary work stoppage aimed at forcing management to accept union demands is known as a:
    a. Strike
    b. Sickout
    c. Slowdown
    d. Boycott

Match the Terms and Concepts with Their Definitions

A.	401(k) plan	Z.	job sharing
B.	arbitration	AA.	job specification
C.	attrition	BB.	knowledge-based pay
D.	bonus	CC.	labor federation
E.	boycott	DD.	labor unions
F.	business agent	EE.	layoffs
G.	cafeteria plans	FF.	locals
H.	collective bargaining	GG.	lockout
I.	commissions	HH.	mandatory retirement
J.	compensation	II.	mediation
K.	contingent employees	JJ.	national union
L.	diversity initiatives	KK.	orientation programs
M.	electronic performance monitoring	LL.	pay for performance
		MM.	pension plans
N.	employee assistance programs	NN.	performance appraisals
O.	employee benefits	OO.	picketing
P.	employee retention	PP.	profit sharing
Q.	employee stock-ownership plan	QQ.	quality of work life (QWL)
R.	flextime	RR.	recruiting
S.	gain sharing	SS.	replacement chart
T.	glass ceiling	TT.	retirement plans
U.	human resources management	UU.	salary
V.	incentives	VV.	sexism
W.	injunction	WW.	sexual harassment
X.	job analysis	XX.	shop steward
Y.	job description	YY.	skills inventory

ZZ. stock options
AAA. strike
BBB. strikebreakers
CCC. succession planning
DDD. telecommuting

EEE. termination
FFF. wages
GGG. worker buyout
HHH. work-life balance

_____ 1. Specialized function of planning how to obtain employees, oversee their training, evaluate them, and compensate them

_____ 2. Efforts to help employees balance the competing demands of their personal and professional lives

_____ 3. Overall environment that results from job and work conditions

_____ 4. Discrimination on the basis of gender

_____ 5. Invisible barrier attributable to subtle discrimination that keeps women out of the top positions in business

_____ 6. Unwelcome sexual advance, request for sexual favors, or other verbal or physical conduct of a sexual nature within the workplace

_____ 7. Programs and policies that help companies support diverse workforces and markets

_____ 8. Scheduling system in which employees are allowed certain options regarding time of arrival and departure

_____ 9. Ability to work from home or other remote locations using telecommunications technology

_____ 10. Splitting a single full-time job between two employees for their convenience

_____ 11. Workforce planning efforts that identify possible replacements for specific employees, usually senior executives

_____ 12. A planning tool that identifies the most vital employees in the organization and information about their potential replacement

_____ 13. Efforts to keep current employees

_____ 14. Non-permanent employees, including temporary workers, independent contractors, and full-time employees hired on a probationary basis

_____ 15. Process by which jobs are studied to determine the tasks and dynamics involved in performing them

_____ 16. Statement describing the kind of person who would be best for a given job—including the skills, education, and previous experience that the job requires

_____ 17. Process of attracting appropriate applicants for an organization's jobs

_____ 18. Sessions or procedures for acclimating new employees to the organization

_____ 19. A list of the skills a company needs from its workforce, along with the specific skills that individual employees currently posses

_____ 20. Evaluations of employees' work according to specific criteria

_____ 21. Real-time, computer-based evaluation of employee performance

_____ 22. Money, benefits, and services paid to employees for their work

_____ 23. Fixed cash compensation for work, usually by yearly amount; independent of the number of hours worked

_____ 24. Cash payment based on the number of hours the employee has worked or the number of units the employee has produced

_____ 25. Cash payments to employees who produce at a desired level or whose unit (often the company as a whole) produces at a desired level

_____ 26. Cash payment, in addition to regular wage or salary, that serves as a reward for achievement

_____ 27. Employee compensation based on a percentage of sales made

_____ 28. The distribution of a portion of the company's profits to employees

_____ 29. Plan for rewarding employees not on the basis of overall profits but in relation to achievement of goals such as cost savings from higher productivity

_____ 30. Incentive program that rewards employees for meeting specific, individual goals

_____ 31. Pay tied to an employee's acquisition of knowledge or skills; also called competency-based pay or skill-based pay

_____ 32. Compensation other than wages, salaries, and incentive programs

_____ 33. Flexible benefit programs that let employees personalize their benefits packages

_____ 34. Company-sponsored programs for providing retirees with income

_____ 35. Generally refers to traditional, defined benefit retirement plans

_____ 36. A defined contribution retirement plan in which employers often match the amount employees invest

_____ 37. Program enabling employees to become partial owners of a company

_____ 38. Contract allowing the holder to purchase or sell a certain number of shares of a particular stock at a given price by a certain date

_____ 39. Company-sponsored counseling or referral plans for employees with personal problems

_____ 40. Loss of employees for reasons other than termination

_____ 41. Process of getting rid of an employee through layoff or firing

_____ 42. Termination of employees for economic or business reasons

_____ 43. Distribution of financial incentives to employees who voluntarily depart; usually undertaken in order to reduce the payroll

_____ 44. Required dismissal of an employee who reaches a certain age

_____ 45. Organizations of employees formed to protect and advance their members' interests

_____ 46. Relatively small union groups, usually part of a national union or a labor federation, that represent members who work in a single facility or in a certain geographic area

_____ 47. Union member and employee who is elected to represent other union members and who attempts to resolve employee grievances with management

_____ 48. Full-time union staffer who negotiates with management and enforces the union's agreements with companies

_____ 49. Nationwide organization made up of local unions that represent employees in locations around the country

_____ 50. Umbrella organization of national unions and unaffiliated local unions that undertakes large-scale activities on behalf of their members and that resolves conflicts between unions

_____ 51. Process used by unions and management to negotiate work contracts

_____ 52. Process for resolving a labor-contract dispute in which a neutral third party meets with both sides and attempts to steer them toward a solution

_____ 53. Process for resolving a labor-contract dispute in which an impartial third party studies the issues and makes a binding decision

_____ 54. Temporary work stoppage by employees who want management to accept their union's demands

_____ 55. Strike activity in which union members march before company entrances to communicate their grievances and to discourage people from doing business with the company

_____ 56. Union activity in which members and sympathizers refuse to buy or handle the product of a target company

_____ 57. Nonunion workers hired to replace striking workers

_____ 58. Management tactic in which union members are prevented from entering a business during a strike

_____ 59. Court order prohibiting certain actions by striking workers

_____ 60. Statement of the tasks involved in a given job and the conditions under which the holder of the job will work

Learning Objectives—Short Answer or Essay Questions

1. Explain the challenges and advantages of a diverse workforce.

2. Discuss four staffing challenges employers are facing in today's workplace.

3. Discuss four alternative work arrangements that a company can use to address workplace challenges.

4. Identify the six stages in the hiring process.

5. List six popular types of financial incentive programs for employees.

6. Highlight five popular employee benefits.

7. Describe four ways an employee's status may change and discuss why many employers like to fill job vacancies from within.

8. Define the collective bargaining process.

Critical Thinking Questions

1. Discuss the various issues and challenges faced by women in the workplace.

2.   Discuss the various issues mangers face in appraising employees' performance; be sure to discuss the concept of the 360-degree review.

3.   Explain how the Family Medical Leave Act of 1993 and a heightened awareness of *work-life balance* have affected modern organizations.

True-False – Answers

1. True	6. True	11. True
2. False	7. True	12. False
3. True	8. True	13. False
4. True	9. False	14. True
5. False	10. False	15. False

Multiple Choice – Answers

1. A	7. D	13. A
2. D	8. A	14. C
3. B	9. B	15. A
4. C	10. C	
5. D	11. B	
6. C	12. C	

Match the Terms and Concepts with Their Definitions – Answers

1. U	21. M	41. EEE
2. HHH	22. J	42. EE
3. QQ	23. UU	43. GGG
4. VV	24. FFF	44. HH
5. T	25. V	45. DD
6. WW	26. D	46. FF
7. L	27. I	47. XX
8. R	28. PP	48. F
9. DDD	29. S	49. JJ
10. Z	30. LL	50. CC
11. CCC	31. BB	51. H
12. SS	32. O	52. II
13. P	33. G	53. B
14. K	34. TT	54. AAA
15. X	35. MM	55. OO
16. AA	36. A	56. E
17. RR	37. Q	57. BBB
18. KK	38. ZZ	58. GG
19. YY	39. N	59. W
20. NN	40. C	60. Y

Learning Objectives – Short Answer or Essay Question – Answers

1. **Explain the challenges and advantages of a diverse workforce.**
    Smart business leaders recognize diverse workforces bring a broader range of viewpoints and ideas, they help companies understand and identify with diverse markets, and they enable companies to tap into the broadest possible pool of talent. Supervisors face the challenge of communicating with these diverse employees, motivating them, and fostering cooperation and harmony among them. Teams face the challenge of working together closely, and companies are challenged to coexist peacefully with business partners and with the community as a whole.

2. **Discuss four staffing challenges employers are facing in today's workplace.**
    The four challenges identified in the chapter are (1) aligning the workforce with the organization's needs, (2) fostering employee loyalty in a time when most companies can no longer guarantee lifetime employment, (3) monitoring employee workloads and making sure employees are not in danger of burnout, and (4) helping employees find a balance, at least temporarily, between the demands of their personal and professional lives.

3. **Discuss four alternative work arrangements that a company can use to address workplace challenges.**
    To meet today's staffing and demographic challenges, companies are offering their employees flextime (the ability to vary their work hours), telecommuting (the ability to work from home or another location), job sharing (the ability to share a single full-time job with a co-worker), and flexible career paths (the opportunity to leave the workforce for an extended period, then return).

4. **Identify the six stages in the hiring process.**
    The stages in the hiring process are (1) selecting a small number of qualified applicants, (2) performing initial screening interviews, (3) administering a series of follow-up interviews, (4) evaluating candidates, (5) conducting reference and background checks, and (6) selecting the right candidate.

5. **List six popular types of financial incentive programs for employees.**
    The most popular employee incentive programs are bonuses, commissions, profit sharing, gain sharing, pay for performance, and knowledge-based pay.

6. **Highlight five popular employee benefits.**
    The two most popular employee benefits are insurance (health, life, disability, and long-term care) and retirement benefits, such as pension plans that help employees save for later years. Employee stock-ownership plans and stock options, two additional benefits, allow employees to receive or purchase shares of the company's stock and thus obtain a stake in the company. Family benefits programs, also popular, include maternity and paternity leave, child-care assistance, and elder-care assistance.

7. **Describe four ways an employee's status may change, and discuss why many employers like to fill job vacancies from within.**

An employee's status may change through promotion or through reassignment to a different position, through termination (removal from the company's payroll), through voluntary resignation, or through retirement. Employers like to fill vacancies created from such changes by promoting from within for these reasons: The employee has been trained by the company and knows the ropes; it boosts employee morale; and it sends a message to other employees that good performance will be rewarded.

8. **Define the collective bargaining process.**

First, the union negotiating team determines member needs, while the management team tries to anticipate union demands and crafts responses to those demands. Second, the two sides conduct a series of meetings during which they attempt to reach agreement by compromising as needed. Third, if the negotiating process is successful, union leaders present the proposed contract to the union membership for a vote. Fourth, if the contract is ratified by member vote, the contract is then signed by the union and the company.

Critical Thinking Questions - Answers

1. **Discuss the various issues and challenges faced by women in the workplace.**

The statistical picture of men and women in the workforce is complex, and various parties have sliced and diced the data in order to promote a variety of conclusions. However, nearly a half century after the Civil Rights Act of 1964 made it illegal for employers to practice sexism, or discrimination on the basis of gender, three general themes are clear. First, in virtually every profession in every industry and every stage of their careers, women earn less on average than men. Over the past several decades, the pay gap has closed from less than 60 percent to roughly 70–80 percent (depending on the survey), but progress has stalled in recent years. Second, even in occupations that have traditionally been served primarily by women, such as teaching and nursing, women still earn less than men on average. Third, the higher up you go in most corporations, the fewer women you'll find in positions of authority. Although women fill roughly half of all managerial and professional positions in the United States, among Fortune 500 companies, only 15 percent of board members and fewer than 3 percent of CEOs are women. Almost half of Fortune 1000 companies have no women top executives. A lack of opportunities to advance into the top ranks is often referred to as the glass ceiling, implying that women can see the top but can't get there.

With laws against employment discrimination, a society that is much more supportive of women in professional roles than it was just a few decades ago, and strong evidence that companies in which women are given opportunities to lead outperform companies that don't, why do these gaps still exist? In addition to instances of simple discrimination, analysts suggest a variety of reasons, including lower levels of education and job training, different occupational choices, the need to juggle the heavy demands of both career and parenthood, and the career hit that parents often take when they step out of the workforce for extended periods—since more women than men choose to be stay-at-home parents.

Beyond pay and promotional opportunities, many working women also have to deal with sexual harassment, defined as either an obvious request for sexual favors with an implicit reward or punishment related to work, or the more subtle creation of a sexist environment in which employees are made to feel uncomfortable by lewd jokes, remarks, or gestures. Even though male employees may also be targets of sexual harassment, and both male and female employees may experience same-sex harassment, sexual harassment of female employees by male colleagues continues to make up the majority of reported cases. Most corporations now publish strict policies prohibiting harassment, both to protect their employees and to protect themselves from lawsuits.

2. Discuss the various issues mangers face in appraising employees' performance; be sure to discuss the concept of the 360-degree review.

Most human resources managers attempt to answer these questions by developing performance appraisals to objectively evaluate employees according to set criteria. The ultimate goal of performance appraisals is not to judge employees but rather to improve their performance. Thus, experts recommend that performance reviews be an ongoing discipline—not just a once-a-year event linked to employee raises. Employees need regular feedback so that any deficiencies can be corrected quickly.

Most companies require regular written evaluations of each employee's work. To ensure objectivity and consistency, firms generally use a standard company performance appraisal form to evaluate employees. The evaluation criteria are in writing so that both employee and supervisor understand what is expected and are therefore able to determine whether the work is being done adequately. Written evaluations also provide a record of the employee's performance, which may protect the company in cases of disputed terminations.

The specific measures of employee performance vary widely by job, company, and industry. Most jobs are evaluated in several areas, including tasks specific to the position, contribution to the company's overall success, and interaction with colleagues and customers. For example, a production manager might be evaluated on the basis of communication skills, people management, leadership, teamwork, recruiting and employee development, delegation, financial management, planning, and organizational skills.

Many performance appraisals require the employee to be rated by several people (including more than one supervisor and perhaps several co-workers). This practice further promotes fairness by correcting for possible biases. The ultimate in multidimensional reviews is the 360-degree review, in which a person is given feedback from subordinates, peers, and superiors. To ensure anonymity and to compile the multiple streams of information, 360-degree reviews are often conducted via computer. Experts also recommend that 360-degree reviews not be used to set salaries and that reviewers be thoroughly trained in the technique.

Evaluating individual performance is a challenge in organizations where employees work in teams. Assessments by the team leader are important, of course, but they can't always sort out what each member contributed to the overall output, particularly in teams that operate with a great deal of autonomy. A good way to address this problem is to have each team member evaluate his or her own contribution and that of every other team member as well. A manager who oversees the team can then compare all the assessments (which are done anonymously) to look for patterns—who contributes the bulk of the new ideas, who's just along for the ride, and so on.

3. **Explain how the Family Medical Leave Act of 1993 and a heightened awareness of work-life balance have affected modern organizations.**

The Family Medical and Leave Act (FMLA) of 1993 requires employers with 50 or more workers to provide up to 12 weeks of unpaid leave per year for childbirth, adoption, or the care of oneself, a child, a spouse, or a parent with serious illness. Many employees can't afford to take extended periods of time off without pay, but at least the law creates the opportunity for those who can.

Daycare is another important family benefit, especially for single parents and two-career couples. In fact, half of all working families now rely on daycare. Nearly half of all companies now offer some sort of childcare assistance, including flexible savings accounts (which let employees put aside from of their pay for childcare and other services), referral programs, discounted rates at nearby childcare centers, and on-site daycare centers. Although the number of companies with on-site daycare centers remains fairly low, recent research led by Bowdoin College economist Rachel Connelly shows that such facilities don't have to be the financial burden many perceive them to be—and can even generate profits. Moreover, daycare facilities also send a message that the company cares about work-life balance.

Another family benefit of growing importance is elder care, assisting employees with the responsibility of caring for aging parents. Many employers now offer some form of elder-care assistance, ranging from referral services that help find care providers to dependent-care allowances. Some companies will even agree to move elderly relatives when they transfer an employee to another location.